21 November, 2021

To Dad & Bea,

— wonderful Parents
whose goodness &
generosity knows no
bounds.

All my love,

Jackson

Other Works by John David Emens

There Are Always More French Fries at the Bottom of the Bag (2019)
Boom! & Adversity (2018)
WTO Panel Dynamics (2007, 2012)

(All available on Amazon)

THE
Slippery Curse
OF THE
Blessed Life

*Eighty Poems, Inspirational Reflections,
and Helpful Spiritual Nuggets*

JOHN D. EMENS, PHD

WESTBOW
P R E S S®
A DIVISION OF THOMAS NELSON
& ZONDERVAN

WestBow Press books may be ordered through booksellers or by contacting:

WestBow Press
A Division of Thomas Nelson & Zondervan
1663 Liberty Drive
Bloomington, IN 47403
www.westbowpress.com
844-714-3454

ISBN: 978-1-6642-4472-6 (sc)
ISBN: 978-1-6642-4473-3 (hc)
ISBN: 978-1-6642-4471-9 (e)

Library of Congress Control Number: 2021918520

Print information available on the last page.

WestBow Press rev. date: 11/05/2021

To my loving parents: J. Richard, Bea, Mary, and Tom

CONTENTS

INTRODUCTION

In 2018, I published *Boom! & Adversity*; it was a literary sojourn of poetic verse and reflections about a broken man whose physical body was unceremoniously falling apart. After ten surgeries, a broken infected ankle could not be remedied, and the leg came off. Strong antibiotics knocked out the kidneys. The hoofbeats of dialysis were approaching fast, and there was little to be done. Yet, the general thesis of *Boom!* was that bad things are not God's purpose, but we can make them purposeful.

In early 2019, I published *There Are Always More French Fries at the Bottom of the Bag*; this text sported some poetry, but it was primarily a collection of spiritual thoughts and personal inspirational reflections of someone positive, upbeat, and content despite deleterious circumstances. I was now taking dialysis, yet peace and joy continued to prevail.

This project, *The Slippery Curse of the Blessed Life*, is a collection more like the latter. Now two years into dialysis, this author has discovered there is still a richly gratified life in spite of being hooked up to a machine four hours a day, four days a week. Now armed with a prosthesis, I am beginning to learn to walk again, although I must admit at this point, progress has been remarkably, painstakingly slow. The spiritual reflections in this book tend to be more assertive, affirming, and evangelical. The purpose of this book is not only to explore one's faith through writing but to better understand the character, nature, and loving habits of our Lord in general. The book is about relationship, not religion. Faith, not fear. Devotion, not division. Commitment, not contrivance. The promise, not propaganda. The actual Deity, not dry, dusty dogma.

This is a collection of fresh ideas and thoughts about a loving God who gives us peace, joy, and hope. Unfortunately, our world of late has become somewhat embittered with incipient strife and unhealthy division.

The COVID-19 pandemic and political and marked racial unrest have left us with an uncomfortable sense of wide disconnect. So, let us take a deep breath, and make a concerted effort to remember to "keep our eyes on the prize." Let us joyfully dip into this text, and look to the Light, and in the process, be illuminated ourselves. Then we can illuminate others. Amen.

—J.D. Emens
Marion, Ohio
May 2021

John D. Emens, PhD

THE SLIPPERY CURSE
OF THE BLESSED LIFE

We all want a tight, tender, close, intimate relationship with God. And we know our relationship with the Lord—like with anyone else—is a dance; sometimes we dance closely, and sometimes we dance less tightly. But as funny as it sounds, the times we tend to dance most closely are during trials and times of trouble. When life hits the fan, we lean mightily on the Lord and hold fast to His promises. On the other hand, when the waves subside, or when times improve—when we come into a prolonged period of blessing—we tend to hunger less for God and rely less on Him and His promises. We stray. We trust in ourselves and even start to feel our blessings are due to a sense of our upright behavior or our own belief in our personal righteousness. We may even think we deserve our blessings, especially if we have been spiritually dutiful (i.e., reading scripture daily, tithing, attending church, and actively serving). We start looking to His hand and not His face. In short, when blessings flow too much, we may forget the Lord, as King Solomon did. Such is the slippery curse of the blessed life.

Scripture is replete of admonitions of such straying from the Lord. Deuteronomy 28:14 (NIV) reads, "Do not turn away from any of the commands I give you today, to the right or to the left." Proverbs 4:27 (ESV) says, "Do not swerve to the right or the left," or "Do not get sidetracked" (NLT). Even more so, Deuteronomy 8:11 (NLT) says, "But that is the time to be careful! Beware that in your plenty you do not forget the Lord your God and disobey his commands."

What tends to be the "cure" to this drifting or straying? Sometimes the best tonic is a good dose of adversity or a tricky trial. Psalm 119:71 (NRSV) says, "It is good for me that I was humbled, so that I might learn your statutes." When you learn or know this painful truth and have wisdom, then God doesn't need to throw you such curveballs anymore to keep you close. He can unhook the leash and know you will still stay close by His side.

James 4:8 (ESV) reads, "Draw near to me, and I will draw near to you." How do we stay near? By knowing we always need Him—in good times as well as bad. With this wisdom, we can avoid the slippery curse of the blessed life!

LOST TOY

Yikes! He's not under my bed. Nor in the toy box. I scamper outside—sandbox vacant. Must be in Mom's car. Climb over back seat—nothin'! Check basement by TV—nowhere to be found. Must be in closet. Must be in closet! Rummage, rummage, rummage. No luck. Phooey! Maybe I left him at Christopher's? Or maybe he's gone forever. Dull shivers down my spine. GI Joe is MIA, and every cell in my body is screaming somethin' awful!

Ask older sister; she laughs and says he was abducted by aliens. Not funny. Not funny at all. Ask Mom: "Too busy making dinner." Ask Papa: "Reading the paper." Go upstairs to my room and sulk. Nobody cares. Can't have dinner without Joe on my lap, squeezed tightly between my legs. Gotta find him. Got to find Joe.

Tears come. Brittle fabric of my soul now emptied, I go downstairs and take my place at the table. Not hungry. Mom tells me I better eat my vegetables. 'Splain I can't eat without Joe. Papa sternly says, "Grow up! Eat! It's just a doll!" Sister laughs. Anger bubbles over. Fidget sompin' fierce. "Sit still!" Mom snaps. Red in face. Hold back tears. Still not touching the silverware.

Now sent to my room, I go upstairs. Clamber onto bed. Weeping, I wrap my hands and face around pillow. Eureka! Under pillow is Joe! I found him! Elated, I thank God. GI Joe is back from behind enemy lines! Don't know how, but he made it! I tuck him under my shirt and place him next to my heart beating out of my chest. Curl up in a ball. Gentle, sound sleep ensues. Joe is back. All is right with the world.

Philippians 4:6 (NKJV) reads, "Be anxious for nothing." Unfortunately, in this world, we learn to be troubled or shook up at a very early age.

OLD FISHIN' BOAT

I vividly recall the ubiquitous beauty surrounding the small lake in Michigan where I fished as a child. I sat in our old fishin' boat holding my favorite pole—the one with twenty feet of backing on my reel just in case I got a "big one." I would carefully bait my hook with a minnow or a stinky night crawler depending on what the fish were feasting on any given morning.

Some days, I would wait for hours just to get one measly nibble. Other days, I would have a dozen fish in the boat by noon. It all depended on whether Bobby Bass or Penelope Perch got hungry and decided it was snack time. But whether I caught one fish, none fish, or twenty fish, I was content to just calmly sit on the serene waters and feel close—intimately close—to the presence of God the Father. I could feel Him in the cool breeze. I could hear Him in the nurturing waves softly lapping the windward side of the rowboat. I could sense Him in the corners of my heart, gently caressing the sweet depths of my young soul and telling me how He tenderly loved me.

John D. Emens, PhD

Brave Lemmings

Daily life takes courage. We all have our battles. For some, it is just getting out of bed in the morning. For most of us, it is the daily grind: going to work, taking care of the kids, paying the bills, and building up that 401(k) in preparation for the golden years, which may not be in fact quite as golden as we had originally thought.

Some think courage is only demonstrated in obvious or flamboyant ways: on the wartime battlefield, in the corporate boardroom, or in a major sporting event. Perhaps courage is also seen in the people who shine in important but seemingly thankless jobs; these are the snowplow warriors, the EMTs, the badges, the preschool teachers, the sanitation engineers (trash pickup folk), cashiers at twenty-four-hour minimarts, coal miners, graveyard shift factory workers, park rangers, Alzheimer caregivers, fast-food restaurant workers, nurse's aides, paralegals, teaching assistants, custodians, and even clergy. This is all the more true during COVID-19.

It takes courage to just do the job when glamour is not involved. It takes fortitude or pluck to show up, do a job, and do it well day after day. Not all of us can be queen bees. We drive Fords or Hyundais and not BMWs or Lexuses. We consume the Big Mac and not the foie gras. Daily, we feed the dog, mow the lawn, take out the trash, and do the dirty dishes. We watch our pennies, stretch our monthly budgets, and still make it to all our kids' school plays and after-school sporting events. Then there are the infirmed who might be taking their regular chemo and radiation treatments, or folks like me who do the dialysis grind four days a week at five fifteen in the morning.

It is hard not to feel like lemmings or gerbils on one of those circular metal wheels in a cage. Yet we show up for work, put in our time, and do our level best to perform to the best of our abilities every day. It takes courage to do the mundane, tedious job that often goes unnoticed and overlooked—and to do it well.

In "The Builders," Longfellow wrote:

Nothing useless is, or low; Each thing in its place is best; And what seems but idle show strengthens and supports the rest … Let us do our work as well, both the seen and the unseen; Make the house, where gods may dwell, Beautiful, entire, and clean.[1]

Yes, there truly is unspoken glory for the simple or the low man on the totem pole.

---

[1] Henry Wadsworth Longfellow, "The Builders," in *One Hundred and One Famous Poems,* ed. Roy J. Cook (1916).

John D. Emens, PhD

BISCUITS AND GRAVY

This morning, I was making my wife breakfast. I was cooking up some country gravy on the stove. I was waiting for the gravy to boil in order for it to thicken. As I somewhat patiently scanned the top layer of gravy, watching for that first slight nudge of a bubble, it reminded me of fishing for medium-sized bluegill on our family pond down in Southern Ohio as a kid. It would be early morning, and the water would be as smooth as a jar of fresh, just-opened creamy peanut butter. I could hear the morning crickets starting to chirp and the locusts commencing to hum as the morning sun would crest over the hilly escarpment to the east. Mud-squatting bullfrogs would begin to croak as the summer-morning temperature began to rise.

My father and I would be casting flies—called little yellow-tailed sunshine poppers—onto the glass-smooth water and watching for any sign of life: a bubble, a bump, or a swirl on the surface preceding a strike and the gobbling of our little poppers. Then, clutching our ultralightweight rods, we would have a battle on our hands, fighting little eight-to-ten-ounce bluegill tearing through the varicose-blue to light-green waters. Eventually we dragged these pesky poisson to the pond's edge to be unhooked and placed in our creels. Fileted, buttered panfish for dinner tonight! Yum.

It was kind of unfair; it was a man-made pond that years ago we had stocked with itty-bitty bass and bluegill ourselves. This little lagoon was only an acre in size, and it was just teeming with healthy-sized fish; it was literally like shooting fish in a barrel. But we didn't care if it was a fish on every fly. As a kid, it was great fun reeling them in and, of course, being with Dad. For him, it was being outdoors amidst the green grass, slowly blowing trees and crisp, clean, crystal clear water—that and being with his boy and all the good things that go with dragging him away from the omnipresent television set with those addictive Saturday-morning cartoons. Well, that's all folks!

Zoe

It was a cold early March afternoon in Ohio. I was cooking up a hot, greasy hamburger in the kitchen when I noticed my dog Zoe lying near my feet in the corner of the room. She wasn't begging or in want of anything; she just wanted to be near me, and it touched my heart. I called to her, and she jumped up and waddled over to me (she is a thirty-five-pound terrier in what should be a ten-pound dog). I opened the treat box and gave her a bacon curl and an affectionate pat on the head. I smiled as she adroitly snatched the treat out of my hand and troddled off to the living room to devour it in the safety of solitude away from our other pup.

As I watched her excitedly exit the room, it occurred to me how we similarly might want our relationship with our dogs to be like that with us and the Lord. Like Zoe, we should just want to sit at His feet—just wanting to be near Him in His presence. Not asking or begging for things. Just relishing the opportunity to spend quality time with Him. Just soaking in the soft presence of Almighty God.

Truth be known, many times, I get in the "gimme-gimme-gimme" mode with the Lord. Instead of seeking Him and delighting in Him, I am too busy begging for things. As it says in Psalm 37:4: "Delight yourself in the Lord, and He will give you the desires of your heart" (KJV). In Matthew 6:33, the Lord Jesus said, "But seek first his kingdom and his righteousness, and all these things will be given to you as well" (NIV).

The point is to place God in our center and worship Him for Him. Then blessings will flow. In short, we should seek the giver, not the gift. It is so easy to get into a "treat-first" mentality. But, if we, like my dog Zoe, choose to love first, the treats—blessings—will come. We just need to remember from where the blessing comes.

And the flip side of all this is to be thankful at all times. In life, we are more than willing to bless others when we know others appreciate the gift or good service we give them. In Luke 17:16–17, Jesus made it clear how much it meant to Him when the one Samaritan leper (out of ten) came back to thank Him for the cleansing he received. It is critical to seek Him first and then to be thankful for whatever blessings He then chooses to bestow upon us. Besides, if we are not grateful for what He has already given us, how can we expect Him to give us more?

The true quality that drives much of these good behavior traits is simple humility. In our humility, we seek to devotionally approach and worship our Maker, and with equal humility, we thank Him for whatever He provides. Humility doesn't come easily, especially in our modern "me-first" world that tells us to always look out for number one. Yet, if we can come off ourselves and let Him be first, or better yet, our center, we will find the gifts and blessing will eventually come our way even if we don't understand the whys and whens that come as they do. Moreover, if the blessings we seek do not come as we wish, or when we wish, we need to accept that as well with thanksgiving, knowing He knows what is truly best. This is part of the essence of having humility. As a senior elder at my church in England used to always say, "God's will in God's time is not lacking in God's grace."

So, like Zoe, seek to lie at His feet in abject devotion. And be thankful when the blessings come. He is a generous giver, but He is not a vending machine—something to be remembered but easily forgotten. Amen.

John D. Emens, PhD

WILD RIDE

When I was on a college athletic training trip in Florida, my team was visiting Disney World. There was an amusement ride called Mr. Toad's Wild Ride. In the middle of the ride, I got a somewhat feckless inspiration, and I jumped out of the moving car. I crouched down and hid behind some of the artificial foliage only to leap out at teammates as they would pass by in their oncoming cars. Yet, after a few laughs, I realized that now away from my car, I had no idea how I would actually make it outside to the exit to safely leave the ride area. Eventually, after barreling through doorway after doorway in near darkness, I came to the end of the ride and emerged into daylight. After many apologies, I was not kicked out of the amusement park—and I was graciously allowed to remain there for the rest of the day.

In many ways, my jumping off the ride is kind of like what happens to us when we stray in our relationships with the Lord. It is so easy to get off-center and get distracted even if we don't in any way intend to. This can be particularly true with regard to service work, as I have found for myself. Sometimes I get so gung ho about serving the Lord, I forget who and what I am serving. The scriptures say I am to abide—not to go on any ultra-wild ride in trying to do too much. They say we are to "run a good race,"[2] but we need to remember it is a marathon more than a sprint. As we serve, we need to take care of ourselves as much as we need to take care of others. This is something I also learned in seminary, where my professors warned us time and time again of the dangers of "pastor burnout." It is so easy to become "overcommitted" in service.

In some ways, the amusement park metaphor is generally applicable to the walk of faith. As we live, love, and serve, there can be many distractions.

---

[2] Galatians 5:12 (Amplified).

Be it from the world, or our own inclinations, we can easily jump out the car, lose track of our calling, and lose sight of what is in our own best interests and health. We need a certain balance and prudence in our walks to make sure we don't outrun the Spirit. When we do so, we may find ourselves no longer bearing fruit and then wondering why. Abiding is the key—always keeping our eyes on Him—but also being good to ourselves in the process. Putting Him first doesn't mean always putting ourselves last. We cannot serve anyone if we are out of service ourselves. It's not being selfish; it is being smart. We all need good nutrition, exercise, and rest.

So, look to Him—and keep focused on the light. Yes, be ambitious for Him, but take care of yourself too, and by doing so, stay in the car and on the right track. In the long run, healthy, vibrant vines and branches yield the most fruit of all. Amen.

SOMETIMES YES, SOMETIMES NO

When I broke my ankle in 2015 and it became infected, we all prayed for a healing. Family, friends, and dozens of churches all prayed, yet the ankle did not heal, and I lost my leg. The strong antibiotics used to save the leg compromised my kidneys, and then we prayed the kidneys would rebound, but they didn't, and now I am on dialysis. For more than three years, we—hundreds of people—were all praying for me, yet God still said, "No!"

Many times, when we pray, it seems like God isn't listening. When we don't get the outcomes we want or desire, it seems like God didn't answer our prayers at all. Truth is, He did answer our prayers; He just said, "No." This seems to contradict what the Lord said in Matthew 18:19: "[I]f two of you agree on earth concerning anything that they ask, it will be done for them by my Father in Heaven" (NKJV).

The trick is seeing that when you, as a devoted believer, ask in His name, you are also implicitly asking according to His will. And as difficult as it is to swallow, generally speaking, when it ain't in His will, it ain't gonna happen. However, as we grow in the Lord, we become more like Him. Then, the things we ask for are the things He would have us ask for from Him, things like love, patience, wisdom, and discernment. As we ask for those things, we will indeed always receive them in full measure. Asking for things that are not in His will is when we typically get the answer no.

In general, why the no? We don't always know. Sometimes we get denied because of timing. God will give us what we want when He wants to do it; usually that is for our good (granting a sixteen-year-old a jacked-up hot rod Corvette may not be a very good idea). Sometimes He wants us to change part of our lives before He will answer our prayer with a "yes." Once we change, we may get the outcome we desire. This can be frustrating because it smacks of a conditional blessing. Truth be known, it is a conditional blessing. God's love for us is unconditional; God's favor isn't.

Finally, God sometimes simply says no for reasons we will never understand. Why are there tornados, earthquakes, and famine? Why do six-year-old children get cancer? Or to dial it down, why can't we seem to pass the college test or ever get the promotion at work? For these things (and more), we will probably never understand until we eternally pass on and all things become known. Until then, we just have to pray, knowing and trusting that His will—although not always getting what we want—is what will end up being best, even if we cannot understand it at the time.

Interestingly enough, when we look back and recall an old prayer, we often can see the wisdom or logic to the answer from God we received. In hindsight, my physical ailments—losing my leg and kidney failure—have given me the opportunity to write and publish that I never had while working in my college teaching job. Many times, our unanswered prayers that seem bad at the time actually work out for good. We just cannot see it at the time.

The scripture in Romans 8:28 reads, "All things work for good for those who love God and are called according to His purpose" (NKJV). The trouble is sometimes "His purpose" seems not to be our immediate purpose. Then we just have to swallow our pride, dignity, and desires and just say, "Oh, Lord, Your will be done," even if that means losing a leg or giving up one's renal function. Yes, God always answers prayers. Sometimes yes, sometimes no.

BIG RED

I have always had an addictive personality. When I was a kid, I was hooked on Dr. Pepper. I can remember going to the local hobby shop on Arlington Avenue after school; they had an old-style pop machine—the kind with glass bottles. For a quarter, I would grab a pop for the walk home. As I grew up, I became addicted to food, cigarettes, and to some extent, alcohol. I was a "treat king," always stuffing my face with something. Always looking for a quick yum.

It is different now. Now in complete kidney failure and on dialysis, my addictive choices are extremely limited. Hoping to get a transplant means no cigarettes, which I smartly gave up eleven years ago. Alcohol is also a no-no. I have to watch my weight like a hawk, so I cannot eat what I want, especially on a renal diet. And no more Dr. Pepper, which is a dark pop that is high in phosphorus. Besides, with my extremely strict fluid restrictions, I cannot actually drink much of anything at all. Bummer!

However, I can chew gum! Lots and lots of it. I go through about fifteen packs a day. It doesn't obviate my desire for food, drink, and the like, but it sure helps. I stick a whole pack of gum (five slices) in my mouth all at once, and I simply let my gums go to town. Cowabunga!

You know, when I was actively teaching as a college professor, I drove a BMW and then a Lincoln. I was all over town, wearing my sport coats and toting my briefcases. Now, I stumble around with a clunky prosthesis, and my wife drives me around in our very mature seventeen-year-old Honda Civic. But you know what? I know what really matters. I have my faith, my wife, two dogs, and most importantly in the world—I have my manly, macho Wrigley's Big Red chewing gum (and lots of it).

In Luke 18:22, Christ asked a rich ruler to give up all his possessions in order to have the kingdom of heaven on earth. I'm with the Lord with all of that, but please God, just don't take away my Big Red chewing gum—at least not yet!

DIALING IT DOWN

In Matthew 6:25–34, Lord Jesus says, "Stop being perpetually uneasy (anxious and worried) about your life … who of you by worrying and being anxious can add one unit of measure (cubit) to his stature or to the span of his life?" (Amplified). He continues, "So do not worry or be anxious about tomorrow, for tomorrow will have worries and anxieties of its own" (Amplified). Truth be known, in our contemporary, modern, busier-than-a-New-York-minute life, this is easier said than done. It is hard not to worry or be anxious in a world of carjackings and school shootings—let alone not being able to lock up your house without having a security system installed or a front-door camera keeping careful watch. And issues of health, food insecurity, and job loss are running rampant in this pandemic.

Yet, the veracity of this passage of Matthew is clear: Don't worry! What is the key? For Christ it is in verse thirty-three of chapter 6: "But seek first his kingdom and his righteousness, and all these things will be given to you as well" (NIV). This is good news and bad news. The good news is that we know what to do—put the Lord first. The bad news is that it isn't always easy.

How do we put the Lord first? We have to obey the greatest commandment: "Love the Lord your God with all your heart and with all your soul and with all your mind and with all your strength" (Matthew 12:20 NIV). Okay, what does it really mean to love the Lord? Perfect hermeneutics aside, the biblical term "love" (there are four of them in the Greek) generally means commitment, obedience, and sacrifice. John 5:13 tells us, "Greater love hath no man than this, that a man lay down his life for his friends" (KJV). In short, when we are sold out for Christ, we are truly putting Him first. To be "sold out" means we fear (respect and revere), trust, and obey Him. We know what it means to fear and revere Him, and we generally know what we do to obey Him; trusting is the real challenge.

Trust is hard. And it is incorrect to believe that if we put all our trust in the Lord, bad things won't happen to us. Christ himself said in John 16:33: "In this world you will have tribulation" (NKJV). The key is recognizing that He won't always keep you from trouble—but having the knowledge that He will always see you through it. As it says in the Psalms 34:19: "Many evils confront the [consistently] righteous, but the Lord delivers them out of them all" (Amplified). Yet, deliverance doesn't always mean we still get the specific outcome we desire. I had a deadly infection in my ankle bone. The Lord delivered me from my infection; I just had to lose my leg to do it. Ouch!

Trusting God means truly accepting His will regardless of the outcome. It in some ways implies a certain blind faith, which isn't surprising since faith is the opposite side of the same coin as trust. It was with great faith that Daniel (6:23) prayed to the Lord God of Israel against the solemn decree of King Darius; when he [Daniel] was lifted out of the lion's den, "no wound was found upon him because he had trusted in his God" (NIV).

Sometimes we have to trust God even when it makes little or no sense. Abraham trusted God and was willing to sacrifice Isaac—his only natural-born son with Sarah—on the altar as he was so directed from above. When archangel Gabriel told Mary she was to carry God's child, she said, "Behold, I am the servant of the Lord; let it be done according to your word."[3] It must have been fantastic and stunning to Mary, but she trusted and was obedient to the Lord. It says in Proverbs 3:5: "Trust in the Lord with all your heart, and lean not on your own understanding" (NIV). It almost seems like God puts us in situations we cannot control just so He can be in control; He does this to give us opportunities to trust Him and rely on Him. As we develop trust with God, we become more useful to Him, and we learn about His character. In doing so, we also become more like Him, and we develop His character ourselves. Trusting in Him is a mainstay of becoming His likeness, and it helps us be better ambassadors of the Lord on earth.

Moreover, as we trust Him, we discover that the outcomes of situations

---

[3] Luke 1:38 (ESV).

matter less. Yes, we want to pass that test, marry whomever we want, and get that promotion. We want to be cured of that disease, and we want to get our diabetic A1C down; no doubt, we want our kids to stay off of drugs. But all these things—no matter how badly we desire them—must come under the purview of His perfect will whatever that might be. By accepting His will, come what may, we are given the gift of perfect peace: "the peace that passeth all understanding."[4] Hence, with peace, we have the antidote to anxiety. On the other hand, being out of His will increases the likelihood of anxiety and a lack of peace.

So, put God first, trust in Him, and have faith in His deliverance—whatever that might be. Keep your eyes on Him, for even in the worst of storms, you might find He is just sleeping right beside you in your boat, ready to spring into action anytime. He did it for the disciples, and He will do it for you. Your test, as they say, will become your testimony. God first, anxiety last. In short, dial it down.

---

[4] Philippians 4:7 (KJV).

The Slippery Curse of the Blessed Life   19

THEOLOGY, NOT "ME-OLOGY"

Dr. Jeff Schreve once remarked that in one's walk with God, a person should practice "theology, not me-ology." The upshot was that a person should not focus on themselves but rather on the Lord: keeping their eyes on Him and putting Him first. It's true. We live in a me-me-me world; with our little attention spans, we are always looking out for number one. In conversations, we have to do all the talking. We are oh-so-busy writing our own personal blogs and taking selfies. We can't wait to scan our cell phones to find ourselves on Facebook or Instagram. We all want our fifteen minutes of fame; the problem is we want it every single day. All day. Ugh!

We need to get off of ourselves. We need to put the Lord first in our lives and put others ahead of us as well. The second greatest commandment was the Golden Rule, namely to "love your neighbor as yourself,"[5] but that never meant just loving ourselves. Jesus washed His disciple's feet, and that was the model for what we are to do: to serve others and put others before us. We all want to receive, but we only do so according to the scriptures when we give first. He is the vine, and we are the branches, and we are to "bear much fruit."[6] The implication is clear: we must be of use to others and be of use to the Lord. As it reads in James 2:17: "Faith without works is a dead also" (NRSV). No doubt about it, "works" are something we do for others besides ourselves.

So, yes, we do need to take care of ourselves, and, yes, we do have our own issues and problems. But if we spend more of our time and

---

[5] Mark 12:23 (NIV).
[6] John 15:5 (NIV).

John D. Emens, PhD

energy helping others, we might find our own concerns are less worrisome. Remember, Christ was thinking of others when He died for us at Calvary. We may not need to perish, but sometimes helping others takes a little dying to ourselves. It's hard to turn off the playoff football game in the fourth quarter to help our kid with homework. It is a sacrifice to take a personal day off at work to help at a local food bank or to take time out of our lives to take that leadership position at church. Or maybe we have to die to ourselves to carve out time for daily devotionals or morning or evening prayer time—just to give Him glory.

Avoiding "me-ology" isn't just action; it is attitude as well. It comes from the heart and the mind. When you put others first—including the Lord—it is really a simple form of praise. You know you are truly doing it for Him and His glory. Even if it's just putting a fresh coat of paint on the service door of the church recreation building, take stock that it is bringing ample joy to our Maker. We may not be all Michelangelo, but we can serve in the role He has given us, big or small. In the end, that is what makes us feel good inside: feeling useful and having a purpose. His purpose. And for this, we can be truly thankful.

DEAD, DIRTY SNOWFLAKES

It is late March, and the snow is falling. Out like a lamb? Au contraire. It is still morning. There is a wet snow with heavy, spongy flakes plopping down on my crusty, frosted windshield as my wife takes me home after dialysis. Wind is capricious and gusty; our little blue Honda Civic heaves awry to and fro a bit in the breezes. Got the radio on, kicking out some classic rock. Left arm throbs a bit from the punctured access sites from dialysis needles. Little conversation. Look out the window and pass a large, crowded cemetery. Watching the tombstones pass, I wonder how many folks in this hallowed field died from kidney failure before there was the modern-day invention of dialysis. A pity. Cresting snow rests on the assorted headstones and monuments. I pass a large crypt with a bleached white angelic statue at the fore; her head is bowed, as if the heavy, lunker snowflakes were weighing her finely chiseled face downward.

Soon, our car comes to a crowded intersection. The stoplight swinging in the wind is colored patently red. As we wait, I look down at dirty snow pressed up against the roadside curb; it looked sad and violated. I felt anguish for the poor flakes, having once been virgin alabaster pure, only to be betrayed awash by this unkind and insensitive motorway. I wondered if these dead, dirty snowflakes ever made it to heaven or were simply recycled in the clouds for another skydive—perhaps as rain in April. I thought of my own life and wondered about my own redemption. Will I ever get that transplant?

As we left the intersection and drove off, I rested my weary head on the freezing side window and closed my grainy eyes. I started to doze off, and then with a resounding jerk, I caught myself and straightened up. I cleared my throat and stared ahead. We pulled into the alley behind our

John D. Emens, PhD

house. After disembarking in our driveway, I pushed the wheelchair with one leg backward up the icy ramp to the house.

Before going inside, I glanced back one last time, and I thought again of the dead, dirty snowflakes. *Ashes to ashes, snow to snow.* I flashed a wry, wan smile, went inside, and shut the thick, heavy wooden door behind me. Relax. Back home. Dialysis over. Go to bed. Time to sleep it off. Maybe get up in time for dinner. Maybe not.

CIRCUS SHOW

Two years ago last fall, about a month after the amputation of my lower right leg, a good friend of mine came over to my house to visit me. I was in bed with my shortened leg propped up on pillows; he stood beside me.

He leaned over, gently patted my shoulder, and said, "Well, Jack, I just wanted to come over and say hello, and I wanted to reassure you that I don't think you are some kind of, well, a circus sideshow now that you lost your leg."

I gave him a weak smile, and we chitchatted a bit more.

When he got up to leave, and then repeated what he had just told me, namely, "Not to worry, Jack. You are not a goofy sideshow—if you know what I mean."

When he left the house, I was left with my mind puzzling like the Grinch from Dr. Seuss[7] when he heard the "Whos in Whoville" still brightly singing without any Christmas gifts. So, I am not a circus sideshow? Ouch! Go figure.

Sure, when I first decided to amputate the leg on doctor's advice, it felt kinda funny. I knew I would never look the same or be viewed the same, but as my youngest sister said, "Jack, you will still be you!"

After being out in public in the past two years, it is to some extent true. People look at you a bit like you belong in a carnival, and they are ready to toss you in-the-shell peanuts. After a while, you really don't care. But whenever I get that stare down by a child or the typical aversion of eyes by adults, I smile and think of my friend who gave me such kind advice and brotherly reassurance.

---

[7] Dr. Seuss, *How the Grinch Stole Christmas*, Random House (1957).

John D. Emens, PhD

Funny thing is, I have not seen my friend now for nine months. I guess I must have made him uncomfortable. (Maybe I should give him a call and tell him I now have a prosthesis. No worries—the carnival has now left town!).

JOY, PEACE, AND HAPPINESS

We all want and seek to be joyful and happy. And it seems we all pray at times for peace. But what makes us experience these three objectives? The past five years have sharpened my interest in this subject and caused me take pause. Nearly a dozen major surgeries, an amputation, and now being on dialysis—I probably could say without reservation I am not as happy as I was when I was teaching and out and about the town. Yet, I still have joy in my life. The simple things, like a shimmering sunrise or a lively Mozart concerto, soothe me in my in most places. A warm, engaging smile from my wife or a meaningful Sunday with friends—not to mention the pleasant satisfaction that comes from the simple putting pen to paper (although now done digitally)—all of these are so meaningful. And, of course, dogs. Dogs always bring joy! Finally, strumming my six string and singing to the Lord is perhaps the greatest joy of all.

Stepping back, it seems after what I have been through that happiness may come from circumstance, but true joy comes from the soul. It is the metaphysical things, the things you cannot put in a test tube— love, gratitude, compassion, empathy, and feelings of trust, loyalty, or friendship—that touch one's soul. Worldly things, like a new car or a double-cheese pepperoni pizza, bring happiness.

Peace? Peace comes from the spirit but should not be confused with contentment. Many of us, including myself, have had much stuff accumulated, including homes, cars, clothes, tablets, and phones. Those things make us comfortable and to some extent gratified, but they don't necessarily bring peace or tranquility. True peace comes from within rather than from without.

For me, knowing Him is the trick. I understand that even when things hit the fan down here, His steady hand is still on the rudder. Outcomes no

John D. Emens, PhD

longer define me. In the past five years, I have had my hand on a different pulse than my own. Letting go and letting Him be in charge isn't always easy, but it is always the truest way to inner tranquility. The way to "let go and let God" is by trusting, which really underpins the whole ball of wax. There is great inner release when we understand that, truly, the battle belongs to the Lord. By trusting in Him, we can truly "let go."

William Hazlitt wrote, "No young man thinks he ever shall die."[8] With that belief, there is a heady confidence of reckless youth and a mirthful ignorance of the inevitable. With age and suffering, one would think joy and peace might be of less frequent occurrence, yet for me, the opposite is true. With fewer days to go until final splashdown, each moment of life is tenderer, more endearing, and more piercing to the soul—and for that, I am grateful. So, hitch your ride on Him and let the peace begin!

---

[8] From "On the Fear of Death" (1822).

SINFUL: NOUN, VERB, OR ADJECTIVE?

If someone were to ask me if I were a sinner, I would probably respond, "Yes, I am sinful because I am human." I would say this because I am, by nature, imperfect, and I inherently make mistakes and at times, many missteps. The whole notion of "sinner" or "sinful" is a bit soupy because it is, by definition, a noun, a verb, and an adjective. To "sin," is a verb, and by strict definition, is to miss the mark or commit an immoral act. To do so makes one a "sinner," yet "sinner," as a noun, has another understanding. "Sinner" can also be state of being in and of itself intrinsic to humanity. In other words, sinner is to human as cheese is to pizza; you can't have one without the other. And then the term "sinful" is an adjective to describe a person who transgresses. Finally, "sinning" is another example of a verb by being the simple straightforward act of wrongdoing.

The long and the short of it that we need to separate sinner as "wrongdoer" and a sinner as a "wrongbe-er." We all are "wrongbe-ers" in the sense that all of us, at times, "be wrong." This shouldn't be surprising. As Saint Paul writes in Romans 3:23: "All of us have sinned and fallen short of the glory of God" (CEV). This is something we should not necessarily feel bad about; it is inherent in us humans. When we do wrong, we should feel contrition—but not for the simple fact we are imperfect. As they say, the only perfect person we know got nailed to a tree.

This might seem confusing, for Christ himself said in Matthew 5:48: "You must be perfect, as your heavenly Father is perfect" (ESV). Yet, by examining the hermeneutics of the word "perfect," we see it actually does not mean be "without flaw," but rather it means "be complete." How can

John D. Emens, PhD

we—the imperfect—be complete? By joining in relationship with God—the perfect.

So, if ever asked to undertake the "sinner's prayer," or ask Christ into your life, think of yourself simply as human, fallible, and in need of the infallible or the Divine. Don't worry; He's eagerly awaiting your request. In fact, He knew you before you were born. Don't worry—He knows where you live. You find Him, and He will find you! Don't tarry! Eternity awaits!

CON JOB

(Fictitious Story and Characters)

Pastor Pat Willard and his wife sat nervously in their chairs on the forty-second floor of the Chicago Sears Tower. A moment later, three middle-aged men came in wearing expensive suits and toting plush leather briefcases.

The first introduced himself as Raymond J. Stiles, and he was the executive sales VP for CON, the Christian Outreach Network. He said, "Patrick, great to meet you. Congratulations on getting your local show on our national network."

Pastor Pat smiled and said, "Thanks, but it's Pat, not Patrick."

Raymond smiled and said, "Well, we think you will now go by Reverend Patrick; it sounds, er, well, more dignified or distinguished."

Patrick gave a weak smile and shot an uneasy look at his wife, Becky.

Raymond continued, "Patrick, this is Bob Jamison, your new front man—and please meet Samuel Roberts, your promo supervisor."

They all shook hands.

Raymond, a short, portly man with a high forehead, took out some chewing gum and unabashedly popped a thick hunk of it into his mouth. He smiled and said, "Yes, Patrick. Your small-time Minneapolis show has finally made it to the big time. Now it is up to us to market it properly. Now you just listen carefully, and we will explain how it all is going to go down. You will be preaching five shows over two days, and we will break them up into five separate TV episodes per week. Each sermon will be approximately twenty-two minutes. Then we will advertise all the vending items for about five minutes at the end."

"Vending items?" Patrick asked.

"Yes," Ray replied. "You know, we will be packaging your sermons onto DVDs, books, and such."

"Well, I have not written any books," Pastor Pat exclaimed.

Raymond grunted and sweetly said, "Well, don't worry, Reverend. We write 'em for you. We just put your name on it."

Pastor Pat blanched but kept silent.

Raymond continued, "Yes, we will be selling DVDs, books, and hats and T-shirts. We already have the T-shirts made up; they say 'Willard Warriors' on them, and we are going to sell them for a love gift of fifty dollars each—a 700 percent mark-up. Praise God, eh?"

"Fifty dollars? For a T-shirt?" exclaimed Pastor Pat.

Raymond smiled and gently patted Pastor Pat's hand. "Don't worry. Our promo people will package the stuff right good. We just ask the TV viewers to prayerfully consider supporting the show, and they'll end up buying the junk."

Pastor Pat shook his head.

"You got a problem with this, Reverend?" Raymond asked.

Pastor Pat looked down and said, "We never did any of this selling stuff in Minneapolis. We just asked for financial support at the end of the show and listed an address for viewers to send a check."

Raymond grinned, slapped Pastor Pat on the back, and said, "Son, you are in the big leagues now. You gotta sell the Jesus junk to stay on the air—it's just that simple."

Pastor Pat cast his worried eyes on Becky; her mouth was shut, but her eyes were cast down, which meant she was silently praying. After a moment, Pastor Pat said, "Well, Mr. Stiles, can we talk a little about the content of my first few sermons? I was thinking of doing a series on obedience."

Raymond looked down and shook his head. "No, son. We don't talk about obedience unless we use it as a hook line to get people to buy the stuff at the end of the show. No *obedience*, *Hades*, or *serious sin* stuff. We don't talk about those things. Those topics make people sad or upset. Our sermons are to *uplift* our TV viewers, if you know what I mean. That way, they buy more of our stuff."

Pastor Pat started to disagree.

Raymond looked him directly in the eye, and said, "You *do* know what I mean, right, Reverend?"

Pastor Pat squirmed in his seat, swallowed convulsively, and meekly nodded.

"Good!" Raymond exclaimed. "I'm glad we understand each other. Now, all we have left to do is for you to sign the contract." He opened up his briefcase and pulled out a long, thick document. "Now, don't you worry about reading the fine print. All you need to know is on the last page here where it says your salary and where to sign."

Pastor Pat looked down at the salary figure. "Three hundred thousand—a year?"

Raymond smiled and nodded.

Pastor Pat glanced at Becky, and her eyes were open as wide as poached eggs. Then she bit her lip.

Dangling the fountain pen, Raymond cooed, "Just sign here."

Pastor Pat hesitated and then asked, "Mr. Stiles, is there any way my wife and I could talk it over for a minute—you know, maybe pray for a bit before we sign anything?"

Raymond calmly replied, "Sure son. Why don't you take some time and pray all you want. Here is the pen. When you get done talking to the Lord, just sign the last page of document right here and come get me. I will be right outside the door waiting on you."

The three men left the room.

Pastor Pat looked at Becky and nervously shrugged. "Honey, whaddya think?"

Barely looking up from praying, she said, "Pat, I … just don't know. It's a lot of money. It would pay off the house and take care of Virginia and Emma's college tuition … but it just doesn't feel right."

Pat interjected, "But, Beck, if the shows are good—"

"Pat, now even you are calling them *shows*. They are not shows; they are spiritual messages from the Lord!"

Pastor Pat ran his nervous fingers through his thick, jet-black tousled hair. He took Becky's hand and bowed his head in prayer. After a long moment, he opened his eyes. He gave his wife a confident but sad smile, and he calmly ripped up the last page of the contract.

Becky nodded, gave him a hug, and whispered, "I am proud of you. Now that is the man I married."

Pat looked at his wife. "Honey, you know we will have to start over. We canceled our contract with our station in Minneapolis, and they have already filled our slot with someone else."

Becky smiled and said, "Honey, looks like it is now the same for us as it was in the very beginning—preaching from the street corners. But maybe that's where the Lord wants us."

Pastor Pat nodded, flashed a wry, knowing grin, and said, "At least my sermons will be my own."

Becky chuckled and replied, "Maybe you can talk about this whole escapade as a good sermon on obedience—as long as we can sell some cheesy hats and T-shirts out of it."

A smile broke across Pat's face. He gave his wife a kiss on the cheek and calmly said, "Beck, let's get outta here and go home."

Raymond J. Stiles was fit to be tied, but a faithful couple had a calm, peace-filled bus ride back to Minneapolis. Yes, they were two true "Willard Warriors"(without the T-shirts).

GOOD PEOPLE

It would not be far off to say that many people sum up Christian dogma to be "good people go to heaven, and bad people go to Hades." Truth be known, that isn't the case. In actuality, good people do not necessarily go to heaven; forgiven people do.

Christian theology is about a relationship with Jesus Christ in which, through Him, one is granted access to the Father in the heavenly places. It's not a binary take on whether a person gets the thumbs-up or a thumbs-down when they pass away. This doesn't mean that goodness or badness doesn't matter; by no means, both of these relative measures do count. However, it is through faith in Christ that heaven is guaranteed. Luke 10:20 reads, "Rejoice, that your names are written in heaven" (NIV).

When one accepts Christ all his or her wrongdoings are pardoned, and eternity is granted with a clean slate. With forgiveness, believers who are wrongdoers and do-gooders "get in" alike. Theologically speaking, believers who do more "good" may wear a larger "crown" and be rewarded in the afterlife accordingly, but salvation is based on mercy and forgiveness—not an earthly notion of a general accumulation of good deeds.

Imagine two young teens going to a movie theater in the rain. It is closing night, and the lines are long. One well-dressed fellow in line has an umbrella and is kind enough to hold his "brellie" over a group of elderly ladies standing in front of him. Behind this well-groomed teen is a rough-and-tumble-looking chap who trudged up at the last minute. Both teens are at the end of the line; everyone ahead of them gets their tickets and goes in.

When both teens get to the window at the same time, the vendor (a young woman) in the kiosk kindly informs them the show is sold out. There is only one ticket left; only one teen will get in. The well-dressed lad reaches for his wallet only to discover that he forgot his billfold at home. Likewise, the rain-drenched, ill-dressed boy checks his pockets only to find he is also without the necessary funding. Both lads plead their case to the girl at the window as to why each of them should get the admission for that last unused seat—even if they can't pay for it.

The young woman vendor wants to help, but she can't decide. She tries to explain how she really doesn't have the authority to let either of them in without a payment. Finally, to the relief of the young woman, the owner of the theater pops his head into the kiosk and asks what is going on. Once the situation is explained to him, the owner recognizes the rain-drenched, rough-looking kid from the Boys Club. He had invited the boy to come to the show the day before, and he lets the kid into the theater. The owner gives the well-dressed fellow a raincheck and tells him to come back to redeem it for a different show.

In either case, the difference was not really money or tickets but the rough young dude knowing the owner of the theater and having some type of prior relationship with him. Likewise, when one is in relationship with Christ, one has a place reserved for them in heaven. In the story, the young lad may have done wrong, stolen, or had an arrest record for all we know, yet the owner had chosen to overlook all his misdeeds and give the kid an entry ticket because a prior commitment and preexisting arrangement had already been made. Heaven isn't for the perfect or necessarily good—just for the forgiven and the known.

THE BULLFROG

The iconic, mature bullfrog nestles smartly in the marshes and awaits its prey. Be it an insect or even a small bird, this baritone croaking amphibian can lunge and snatch either of them out of the air. The coarse fabric of his almost grotesque skin is greenish brown, and it camouflages nicely with the vert flora near the mossy water's edge. Thick, powerful haunches propel these surprisingly large beasts toward helpless quarry in the blink of an eye. Nocturnal predators, the bullfrog lethargically snoozes daily in the warm oozing mud or hides deep in the shadows of cattails bogs.

Full-grown bullfrogs rule the roost; they call their own shots. Comely or winsome they are not, but around the lake or pond, beauty contests seldom are the order of the day. The bullfrog is exactly what he is supposed to be: a million-year reptilian survivor and small creature of God. He was designed to be a cold-blooded killer in both senses of the word. With no conscience, he feasts on prey with no remorse. Not a thinking machine, he operates instinctually and exists totally in the moment. No worries about yesterday or fretting about tomorrow—that we could be so fortunate.

John D. Emens, PhD

NEUTRAL

We Christians typically perceive the world with binary thinking: right or wrong, positive or negative, good or evil. In truth, although there are many things and situations in which something is definitely "good" or "bad," or "right" or "wrong," much of the time, there may be a gray area or something I would call "neutral." Life can be complicated, and simple interpretations, although compelling, may not be appropriate. In "theo-babble," we call pulling thoughts, understandings, and interpretations out of the Bible into our physical lives *exegesis*. On the other hand, when we read what's going on in the world into the Bible or biblical principles, we call it *isogesis*, and this is where we can get into trouble.

Let me give an example. I live in an older house built just after the Second World War. Like any older home, it has some issues, but my wife and I recently had kind of a doozy. The trouble was specific and chronic; the electricity in our house would go on and off without rhyme or reason. Most the time, it was fine, but it would go through stretches where the kitchen in particular would "wink out" for no reason.

We have a very smart handyman who works on the house, and he was completely stymied. We then hired a very experienced electrician who also could not fathom the problem. It always seemed like when the electrician was at the house, the problem did not materialize. The electrician said he couldn't fix something when he couldn't specifically locate the difficulty. The problem continued and was at that point quite maddening. I became convinced there were dark or perhaps evil forces at work, and I prayed fervently for divine intervention to find a solution to the problem.

One night, when the lights went out, I jumped on my smartphone and called the electrician. He rushed over, and with the lights out, he could make a proper diagnosis. It seems there was a very complicated situation where there was an intermittent circuit problem in the house and a loose electrical hookup on the telephone pole outside of the house. The problem had been twofold. The solution was for the electrician to do rewiring of the electrical circuitry on the side of the house and the city power company to fix the electrical couplings at the telephone pole.

Eventually, it all got sorted out. Repairs were made to the house, and the power company fixed the relays up on the telephone pole. In the end, it was much ado about nothing. But it taught me an important lesson: don't read everything in the world around us from a simple spiritual lens of good or evil or right or wrong. It is so tempting to put the complex empirical world around us into neat, tidy, and simple spiritual boxes; this is so easy to do, and we do it all the time.

This is not to say we should not use wisdom and discernment in understanding the world around us. I do not dispute the fact that evil does exist in the world, but many situations and difficulties in life—like the electrical problem in our house—are not spiritual or metaphysical. Instead, they are neutral, and once they are practically explained, they are quite understandable. Simple thinking is good. Overly simplistic thinking is not, and it can be misleading or even dangerous. Like with our house electric boogeyman problem, it can make you feel downright silly when the truth is finally revealed.

John D. Emens, PhD

THIRST

I have a dry, parched tongue. Often, my taste buds are like a crusty old bathroom sponge. A stale mouth like dry, old, crinkly potato chips. I chew gum ubiquitously to compensate. Sometimes I use hard candy. I dream of cool, crisp, cold streams of mountain spring water or a frosty mug of ice-cold root beer or Pepsi. Nope, not for me.

Yep, I am on a fluid restriction because of dialysis. Thirty-two ounces of water a day. That's it. Every other day, I weigh in to check my fluid levels before they put the lines in and suck my blood for four hours to keep me kicking for another day. Oh, boy!

Still wondering why this all happened. Didn't sign up for this. Guess I'll find out when I reach the other side. In John 16:33, Christ said, "In this world you will have trouble" (NIV). He didn't say anything about being parched.

HUMMER TRUST

(True story—names have been changed.)

There is a good and reasonably priced restaurant in the town I live in. The food is tasty, and the service is excellent. Before my accident when I shattered my ankle five years ago, it was one of my weekly haunts. Between classes, I would frequently grab a bite and sometimes sit in the corner during slow hours and do some grading or prep work. Most days, the owner would come by and say hello. Jerry would sometimes sit down with me, and we would shoot the breeze and catch up, usually telling a quick joke or the latest quip or whatever newsy morsel was going around.

Jerry is middle-aged and has dark, tousled hair and a high forehead. One day, he came over rather excitedly to my table. He explained that he had just purchased a new car, and he was dying to show it to me. I nodded, and we went outside. It was a clear crisp unseasonably warm autumn day, and lo and behold, Jerry walked up to a slick silver-gray Hummer H2. Now that was a car! I paced around the mid-sized beauty and sang its praises, which was easy to do. It was music to Jerry's ears.

After a moment, Jerry glanced at me and smiled. He pulled the car keys out of his suede leather jacket and said, "Want to take it for a spin?"

I hesitated, almost a bit nonplussed, since Jerry and I were only really restaurant acquaintances and not at all particularly close friends.

Jerry proudly said, "I insist."

So, I took the keys and got behind the wheel. It was all black leather trim, and it had that great new car smell. I shut the door, and Jerry motioned for me to roll down the window. He said, "Make sure you take it out on Route 23 and really wind it up! Have fun!"

I said, "Are you not going to ride with me?"

John D. Emens, PhD

Jerry calmly replied, "Nah. Just go for it. Take your time. I trust you."

As I pulled out of the restaurant parking lot, I had two feelings. One, I was excited to give this new ride a whirl. I had never driven a Hummer before. Even more so, I was touched and really moved that Jerry would trust me that much with his brand-new vehicle. I felt good to be that honored and relied upon with a spanking-new, $80,000 car that was not my own.

Truth be known, I was like a kid in a candy store. I cranked up the radio and opened the sunroof—even though it was late September. I took it through town, and then per Jerry's suggestion, I took it out on the highway and stomped the pedal down giving it some "wellie" (as they say in England) just for good measure. Totally impressed, I brought the car back unscratched to Jerry and thanked him profusely for the test drive.

It feels good to be trusted, and this is a lesson we can learn in our relationship with the Lord. Just as we like to be trusted, He likes to be trusted—and He bestows favor upon those who do. As it says in Psalm 91:14: "I will set him on high, because he knows and understands My name [has a personal knowledge of My mercy, love, and kindness—trusts and relies on Me, knowing I will never forsake him, no, never]" (Amplified). Or in the book of Daniel (6:23) where when he was lifted up out of the lions' den, "no wound was found on him because he [Daniel] had trusted in his God" (NIV). When Abraham was willing to trust God even at the life of his own son Isaac, God rewarded him by making him the "father of many nations."[9]

God is a person, or persons, really. He has feelings. Remember He made us for Him, and I would hazard to guess that nothing makes Him feel better than to know and feel that we, His children, truly trust in Him. There is also reciprocity in trust; for in His knowing we trust Him, He also knows we want to please Him, and therefore, He can trust us. That makes us more useful and more dependable to Him. Trust and the desire to please Him are the bulwark for developing obedience, which is one of the hardest, but most important virtues to develop. Love, trust, and obedience are all the mainstays of good, healthy parent-child relationships on earth—we know this—and it is also true with us and God.

In closing, Jerry's trusting me with his new Hummer was the beginning

---

[9] Romans 4:8 (NIV).

of a stronger, closer friendship. He eventually introduced me to his family, and he even took his daughter to some of my college classes. I prayed with the family on many occasions, especially when Jerry's mother took to an illness and then her eventual passing. In the end, I guess by Jerry trusting in me with his car, he learned he could trust me with things even more important and precious to him—namely, his family—in good times and bad. Our friendship started with an automobile, and it ended with Jesus Christ. Amen.

Summer Sled Ride

(True story—David is not his real name.)

My family has a summer house on a small lake near the tiny town of Cedar in the upper portion of the lower peninsula of Michigan. We spent summers there swimming, skiing, boating, sailing, fishing, and golfing. Winter activities were sledding, snowmobiling, ice skating, downhill skiing, and cross-country skiing. Fond midsummer memories with lakefront chums of sundown campfires on the shores of nearby Lake Michigan and climbing and running down the steep Sleeping Bear Dunes in the nearby town of Glen Arbor. Cherry picking and strawberry picking, and late-night star gazing until the wee hours. Truly heaven on earth.

One of my most interesting memories occurred when I was about fifteen. I was racing my lake buddy David on the Timberland downhill summer jet-sled course. The course was made up of a series of downhill curvy ramps on what was in the wintertime an actual slalom snow skiing hill. The course had high-banked curves like you see in luge or bobsled races in the Olympics, and the jet-sleds that we rode reached remarkable speeds, perhaps up to forty-five miles an hour. There were two courses side by side so that participants could race each other down the hill. The course was half a mile long, and at the end of the big hill, there was a straightaway where the users could apply the brakes to the jet-sleds in order to slow down and safely coast to the finish.

On this particular day, it was closing time. It was the last run, and David, a six-foot-six lad with patently blonde hair, had been dueling me all day. David was two years older than me, and we frequently competed in all our sports from skiing to fishing to sailing. I was a gangly six-foot-two, and my knees hit my chest on the jet-sleds as I bent low to avoid air drag as I hurtled down the ramp.

Since it was the last run of the day, both of us knew we were going to go for broke. I decided from the beginning of the run I was not going to use my brakes at all the whole way down, which was downright foolish. Halfway down the run, I was in the lead, but near the end, David was closing fast. As we approached the straightaway, I stared down David—we were in a dead heat. Both of us chose not to use our brakes at all as we closed in on the finish. As we plunged headlong down the closing ramp, side by side at breakneck speed, neither of us paid much attention to the two-foot upright steel metal post that was blocking the end of the course (the post served as a protective barrier so that jet-sled riders couldn't go off the ramps and into the concession area).

Side by side, we hurtled down the finishing area of the ramps. I was winning by a nose when I looked up at the last minute to see my jet-sled slam into the metal post. The jet-sled flipped up into the air as did I, and I landed unceremoniously in the middle of the concession area. I had been flung in the air about twenty feet past the end of the ramp.

When I got my bearings and looked around, I saw David on his back next to me, and his sled was draped over across his lower body. Startled, our eyes met, and when we discovered neither of us were seriously injured, we broke out into inane laughter. As we slowly picked ourselves up off the ground, the owner of the facility rushed over to make sure we were okay. In the end, neither David, nor I, nor the jet-sleds were harmed or damaged; in Shakespearian fashion, all's well that ends well.

More recently, it has occurred to me that the jet-sled races down the ski hill ramps are kind of metaphor for life. We get so caught up in the competitive rat race of life that we sometimes get blindsided by an unexpected finish. None of us knows or can predict "for whom the bell tolls,"[10] or when our physical lives may end, abruptly or not. I, for one, want to make sure I am at peace with my Maker before I expire. Although

---

[10] Ernest Hemingway, *For Whom the Bell Tolls*, 1940.

John D. Emens, PhD

I don't pay much heed, many say the world, especially in this pandemic, is in the end-times because there are "wars and rumors of war ... earthquakes and famine" as the scriptures intuit.[11] Perhaps we should all take pause; when He does return, we might all do ourselves a favor if we are on the right side of the ledger. Amen.

---

[11] Matthew 24:6–7 (NIV).

SUMP PUMP

My wife and I live in an older home in a lower-water-level area of Marion, Ohio. When it rains, particularly in the spring, our basement tends to accumulate water. Fortunately, we have our handy-dandy sump pump that keeps our basement from flooding. Our sump pump is sturdy and reliable, and it is the one thing keeping the water levels down to avoid ruining our furnace in a flood. During a particularly hard rain, I can hear the pump kick on every two or three minutes all night long. So far—knock on wood—the sump pump has never malfunctioned, and in ten years living in this house, we have never have had any serious flooding problems. But time and again, it has occurred to me what might happen if the electric power would go off for any extended period of time. In such case, the sump pump would not operate, and the basement would no doubt fill with water. Time to call Servpro!

It occurred to me that sump pumps are kind of a metaphor for our lives in Christian service. We go about our lives doing our best to balance putting food on the table while putting Christ first or in the center of our lives. We want to be like that sump pump, chugging along dutifully and reliably in how we serve our Lord, yet we need to balance abiding in His strength and His power and not that of our own. We want to carefully be in His will; in doing so, He will give us the means and wherewithal to complete the tasks He has for us to accomplish. If we stray, our branches will no longer be connected to the vine, if you will, and we will wither and fall short. The sump pump fails. If we run our race correctly and abide closely, we work in His power and His strength, and there is very little we cannot do.

Our days are hectic and cacophonous. We need to stop and listen for the still, small voice of the Lord in the maelstrom of life. We need to seek

Him in earnest. He says, "You will find me when you seek me with all your heart."[12] In His will, His power will keep our sump pump working to accomplish all He has for us to do in His way and His time. Otherwise, we are serving in our power only, which we know may shut off at any time; in such "shut-off" times, we cannot serve Him. We can only be salvaged by Him.

With our ears cocked up toward Him, let's keep our heads above water and be the serving professionals, avoiding disaster, so as to not need any imaginable kind of Servpro at all! Amen.

---

[12] Jeremiah 29:13 (NIV).

THE SHORT BUS RIDE HOME

(This is a story I heard in a sermon long ago; this
rendition is mine. Names are fictitious.)

It was a cool, crisp, sunny October afternoon outside Fort Collins, Colorado. William C. Richardson was driving on his typical bus route, dropping off the kiddos after their daily schooling. It was a "short bus," meaning that the children on his route were "challenged," which to Bill only meant they were special. As he drove, Mr. Richardson thought about his own son Tommy, who was seven years old. Bill smiled; his son was into pee wee football, and the little tyke was good at it. The coach of his team called his son "Touchdown Tommy" because the child always seemed to have a nose for the ball and the end zone. Thinking of his son, Bill smiled; he was so proud.

It was getting near the end of his route, and he only had six more kids to drop off. He approached Russell Park on the right, which had a sharp curve next to a dangerous mountain cliff. Bill always slowed down on this part of the route. As he came to the elbow of the curve, he saw a rabbit dart out of the bushes across the road in front of the bus.

As Mr. Richardson swerved the bus a bit to the left, it occurred to him how odd it was that a rabbit would come running out of the bushes in the late afternoon. Then he immediately saw why: a large black dog—maybe a Lab—was chasing the bunny out into the road in front of him. Not wanting to hit the dog, he yanked the bus to the left, and the vehicle then fishtailed dangerously and careened toward the cliff.

Bill quickly pulled the steering wheel to the right and yelled, "Hold on, kids!" Tires screeched, and kids screamed (mostly in delight). The bus fishtailed the other way and was heading right into the park. The bus jumped the curb with a bang and barreled through a four-foot hedge going thirty miles an hour. Just before the bus hit the hedge, there was another large thump. What looked like a large red-and-white checkered picnic basket went up in the air and flew off to the right of the bus and landed with a dull thud. Bill glanced up and saw his careening bus was approaching a playground. He slammed on the brakes, and the bus veered onto the grass and eventually hit gravel. Forty yards later, the bus skidded to an abrupt stop with dust and dirt kicking up everywhere.

Mr. Richardson put the bus in park, and he quickly glanced backward to check his young bus riders; they were sprawled everywhere throughout the vehicle. Even though he was a big man, Bill deftly pounced up and tended to them right away. He calmed them down, and then got them off of the bus, one by one. By now, they were all crying and profusely carrying on. He set them down in the grass in a big circle and checked them over. It looked like Missy had a bloody nose, and Colin might have hurt his arm. The other four kids looked all right except for some bumps and bruises. He got out the first aid kit and began to administer some relief when he heard the sirens.

Ambulances and two fire trucks soon pulled up beside them onto the grass. The EMTs and first responders got to work. Bill leaned up against the bus and lit up a cigarette. Sweat was pouring out of his body like Niagara Falls. There was a cool breeze, and Bill loosened his shirt and rolled up his sleeves. He clenched his fists, and his eyes were moist. With a furrowed brow, he fought back tears.

An hour later, the scene had calmed down considerably. Parents had come and picked up the children. Colin had to go the emergency room for a broken humerus, but the rest of the kids were all right. The state highway patrol and the city police were taking down the report.

There was one ambulance left, and there was a small stretcher placed with one fatality—a small boy. They asked Mr. Richardson if he knew who the young lad was, and Bill nodded and got into the back of the ambulance with the deceased child; the doors were shut, and the ambulance drove away.

As the ambulance pulled away, the state trooper scratched his head. He turned to the city cop and said, "Sir, do you know why the bus driver got into the ambulance with that small boy who was killed at the scene? I mean, that kid wasn't even on the bus. He was the one playing in the park."

The city inspector looked down at the ground for a moment, cleared his throat, and quietly replied, "Yes, because that was the bus driver's own son."

The trooper shook his head and spat on the ground; in disbelief, he said, "You mean that bus driver ran over his own kid to save all the children on the bus?"

The city inspector nodded and said, "That's about the size of it."

The trooper shook his head again and said, "Couldn't he have just swerved one more time to try to miss the boy?"

The city inspector said, "I know Bill Richardson well. He knows what he did, but he must have felt it was absolutely necessary. He must feel awful, but he also knew where his responsibilities lay. His job was to get those kids home safely, and that was what he was going to do."

The trooper exclaimed, "And that meant running over his own son?"

The city inspector replied, "If need be. If need be."

The state trooper said, "That bus driver is some kind of man."

The city cop replied, "Yes, He is that indeed."

What is the lesson for us? Well, if we look at this story metaphorically, we humans are the children in the bus, and God the Father is Bill Richardson, the bus driver. Humanity is represented by the bus going off the cliff. The only way for God the Father to save us humans from going off the cliff and get us safely into the park—heaven—was to run over His own Son. That was the only way God the Father felt he could guarantee everyone could make it to "safety" in heaven. This just shows us how much God the Father loves us and how much Jesus Christ loves us too. As we know, the Lord did not try to flee. He accepted His cross, His death, voluntarily. As Christ said the night before he died, "Father, if you are willing, take this cup from me; yet not my will, but yours be done."[13]

You know, they say in a wartime situation, it is harder for a parent to watch their own child be tortured than to be tortured themselves. At Easter, we celebrate Jesus for what He did; in my view, we need to celebrate God the Father for what He did too. He placed His own Son in harm's way and watched Him die a slow, agonizing death just to ensure our salvation. Never doubt a Father's love. Amen and amen.

---

[13] Luke 22:42 (NIV).

BLUETOOTH

(Fictional story)

Manny Rodrigues was fourteen when his family emigrated from Guatemala to the United States. At the age of sixteen, he got a job as a line cook at a family restaurant in Phoenix, Arizona. Manny was the low man on the totem pole, only serving soup and biscuits and occasionally making salads. He was hardworking and industrious and wanted to move up in the business. His goal in life was relatively modest: he wanted to someday have a happy family and own a nice SUV.

Manny was big in stature for a Guatemalan, about six foot two, and he weighed about four hundred pounds. His thick, dark hair was long, and he had to wear a hairnet at work. Coming from a poor immigrant family, his clothing was not the finest. He nearly always sported a five o'clock shadow from not shaving, and his general hygiene was questionable. Yet, Manny was smart. He knew he needed some kind of an advantage, some way to stand out, if he were to ever get ahead in the business.

One day, he had a bright idea; he got himself a Bluetooth ear telephone. He gave the phone number to his boss at the restaurant. All the other cooks and employees at the restaurant laughed at Manny and his Bluetooth, but his boss loved it. Throughout the workday, his boss would use the Bluetooth to page Manny for just about anything at any time. Manny was soon filling the ice containers at the salad bar. Sweeping the restaurant. Taking out the trash. Cleaning the parking lot. Soon the boss became dependent on Manny; whatever pedestrian job needed to be done at the restaurant, the boss would call Manny on his Bluetooth, and Manny would eagerly jump to it. Manny promptly performed his jobs, and he did them well.

Soon Manny was line supervisor, and then he was promoted to crew chief in the kitchen. After two years in the kitchen, the boss found out Manny had a knack for numbers, and he put Manny on the register out front. Manny, who had saved up most of his earnings, went out and bought two nice outfits and a double-breasted blue blazer. He cleaned himself up nicely, and he began wearing his nice clothes to work. Soon, Manny was put on as floor supervisor over all the waiters and waitresses.

A year later, he was made assistant manager. When he got the promotion, Manny went out and bought himself a GMC Acadia, and he paid cash for it. Manny worked at the restaurant for six more years. He saved all his money, and at the age of twenty-four, he rented a small building on the east side of town and opened his own restaurant. He insisted that all his employees wear Bluetooth phones; his employees became the most industrious and efficient workers in town. Soon, the restaurant was making money hand over fist.

Manny bought a nice home on the affluent east side of town, and he paid cash for it. A year later, he met a nice woman also from Guatemala; they got married and had two children. By the time Manny was thirty, he had five restaurants. All his businesses were so successful that the city newspaper wanted to do an article on him. When the reporter asked him about the secret to his success, he humbly responded, "Hard work and my Bluetooth."

The reporter chuckled and said, "Bluetooth?"

Manny explained how he had used his Bluetooth to work his way up in the business, and that now, all his employees wore them. The reporter was no longer laughing.

Meekness is not weakness. Yep. "Blessed are the meek: for they shall inherit the earth" Matthew 5:5 (KJV).

John D. Emens, PhD

SINCERITY, HONESTY, AND THE TRUTH

These days, it seems like anything and everything is negotiable. Be it an iPhone contract, a sports car, or a college football ticket, all these things can be bargained for. Yet, these examples are all "things;" it is easy to bargain or negotiate for the empirical. Similarly, we also seem to dicker with the metaphysical; sincerity, honesty, and the truth all seem to be negotiable. There are few rights and wrongs. Lots of gray. No absolutes. Justice depends on who you know and how expensive an attorney you can hire.

In fact, there is at present so much pretense and duplicity that anytime we hear anything that smacks of sincerity, we confuse it with the truth. Just because someone honestly believes something with all their heart doesn't make it true; for more than a millennia, man honestly, truly, believed the world was flat, but that didn't make it so. Moreover, there is almost a consensus that anything we cannot wrap our minds around simply cannot be. The concept of heaven seems to be too vague and ambiguous and simply be wishful thinking; the idea of Hades so unthinkable it must be untrue because such things simply could not be compatible with a loving, compassionate God. Most of the modern world pooh-poohs heaven as a simply being a silly supper table in the sky, and they laugh at the idea of a Day of Judgment, but this doesn't make it untrue or not so.

We live in a world where *moderation* is the norm. Avoid the extremes, and as long as one fits in the middle, everything will be all right. The problem is that truth doesn't care about the middle. There isn't really safety in numbers. Sooner or later, no matter how hard we squeeze, the tube of toothpaste does run out—and our physical lives will end. This is an incontrovertible fact. The good news is we all have an eternal spirit and soul. God gave us this. The question, then, is when we pass away, where and with whom will we be spending eternity?

Sincerity and honesty are good and desirable, but the truth is inevitable. Let us not deceive ourselves!

John D. Emens, PhD

Being Perfect

A lot of people think being a Christian is about being a perfect, sweet person in an imperfect world. The word *sweet* is pure subjectivity, but *perfect* is not. Christians are not perfect, and neither is anyone else. As it says in James 3:2: "For all of us make many mistakes" (ISV). Okay. Some might say Christians are more *holy*, but that is more about what we should attain and not necessarily what we are. Holiness smacks of *perfection*, but it has little to do with its true meaning. *Holy* by definition means "set apart," "separate," or "sacred," not something mystical or ethereal. God wanted Israel to be a "holy" nation, namely to be "set apart" for Himself. Moreover, God calls Himself a "jealous" God, and He wants each one of us of in some way to be "set apart" or "holy" in our relationship with Him.

Being perfect? Well, Jesus did say in Matthew 5:48: "You therefore must be perfect, as your heavenly Father is perfect" (ESV). But the word *perfect* in the Greek translation means to be "complete." How can we be complete? Not being without flaw or ever committing a mistake or error. We are complete by being in a relationship with the Lord our God. When we do make mistakes, we are forgiven, and that makes us complete, whole, plenary, and without blemish in the eyes of the Father. And that is why we will be with Him forever.

SAILBOATS

God warns us time and time again not to "harden our hearts" or let "our hearts turn cold." Yet, what is even worse is becoming indifferent, ambivalent, or uncommitted. He says in Revelation 3:16: "So because you thou art lukewarm, and neither hot or cold, I will spew you out of my mouth" (ASV).

You see, to God, we are like sailboats. When we don't care, we are like a sailing craft with no wind; we are dead in the water. We are going nowhere. With no wind, a sailboat cannot be steered either way; nor can we by God. If we are in God's good graces, we can be blessed. If we are going the wrong way, God can throw us a curveball or use a roadblock to get our attention, and thus get us back on track. But if we are totally indifferent, oblivious, or don't care, there is little He can do. God has given us free will, and He has to honor that—even to our detriment.

We all need to be careful and guard our hearts. Solomon was king of all Israel and is said to have been the wisest man on earth; he is responsible for writing the book of Ecclesiastes in the Bible. Yet in his later years, Solomon's heart grew cold and distant, and ultimately, he fell away from the Lord. Enough said.

John D. Emens, PhD

GOD'S PREROGATIVE

They say it is a woman's prerogative to change her mind. Well, according to scripture, the same is true for God. In the book of Exodus (32:9), God was absolutely livid with the Israelites when they made a golden calf as an idol and bowed down worshiping it: "The Lord told Moses, 'Now let me alone, so my wrath may burn hot against them and I may consume them'" (NRSV).

In Exodus 32:13, Moses interceded on behalf of the Israelites and begged God not to destroy them. He prayed to God, "Remember Abraham, Isaac, and Israel, your servants, how you swore to them by your own self, saying to them 'I will multiply your descendants like the stars of heaven, and all this land that I promised I will give to your descendants, and they shall inherit it forever'" (NRSV). Then, Exodus 32:14 reads: "And the Lord changed his mind about the disaster that he planned to bring on his people" (NRSV). Another translation reads: "Then the Lord turned from the evil which He had thought to do to His people" (Amplified).

Similarly, in chapter 18:7–8: The Lord spoke to the prophet Jeremiah, saying, "At one moment I may declare concerning a nation or a kingdom, that I will pluck up and break down and destroy it, but if that nation, concerning which I have spoken, turns from its evil, I will change my mind about the disaster that I had planned to bring on it" (NRSV).

I must admit, sometimes when praying to the Lord, I think of a kind, yet irresolute, unyielding, stubborn God who practices "tough love." He is bound and determined to do His will for my life or others' lives almost regardless of what we may think, pray, or ask. Even in 42:2, Job said, "I know that you can do all things, and that no purpose of yours can be thwarted" (NRSV). Yet, according to the scripture just cited, God can and will change His mind based on what and how we petition Him. This just goes to show a deeper revelation; namely, God truly is a Living God with feelings and mind of His own (duh!). He is not a silly idol made out of stone, metal, or carved wood. Moreover, Moses's request changing God's mind shows the power of intercessory prayer. The Lord does listen to us, and at times, He grants us the favor we seek for the things we want done. This should give us confidence when praying that our petitions and devotions do truly matter. We can pray boldly in earnest, knowing we have a loving Father who is willing to truly listen and consider what we utter.

Take heart! Our prayers do matter. God is listening; whether He grants us our petitions is totally up to Him. But just as He, at times, tries to steer us in one direction, according to scripture, it also possible through prayer for us to change God's mind, and perhaps His favor as well. Do not give up hope—keep praying!

God's Love

How do we love God? How does God love us? Is spiritual love different from love on earth? How can we comprehend the height, depth, and strength of God's personal love for each one of us? Tall order. In some ways, it is hard to define love in a contemporary sense. We use the word *love* ubiquitously. We love pizza. We love sunny days. We love football Sundays. We love going to the cinema. We love our kids, dogs, cats, and pet turtles. I hate to say it, but the word *love* has become hackneyed, stale, almost cliché for nearly everything. It is hard to differentiate the word *love* between liking something, simple affection, infatuation, true physical attraction, and deep sweet tender amour.

In the Greek language, there are four terms for love, but the two that are closest to that used in the Bible to represent God's love are *storge*, which resembles family love, and *agape*, which means unconditional love. In Romans 8:15 (NIV), Saint Paul says when we speak to God, we pray "Abba!" which means "father" or really "daddy." And Paul also writes about God in 2 Timothy 2:13: "If we are faithless he remains faithful" (NIV).

God's love (not favor) is not based on our behavior. No matter how good, bad, or ugly we be or become, He still cares for us just as much. God's love is committed love in the fullest sense of the word. Some people may ask—and this is a good question—how do I know if God truly loves me? This may be a particularly apt question, especially if life has brought you a plethora of hard knocks. You may not have seemed to have seen God working in your life at all. There are three reasonable responses to that question. First, as difficult as it seems, it is important to view God's love outside of good or bad circumstances. We live in a modern-day culture of asking, "What have you done for me lately?" Sometimes it seems God doesn't do anything for us at all. I lost my leg, my kidneys, am on dialysis, and have lost my entire life as I previously knew it. Yet I know God loves me; throughout my ordeal, He has given me His perfect peace. Outcomes did not go my way, but through my affliction, I have grown closer to Him than ever before. Sometimes, in prayer, I feel his joy and good pleasure. My body has gone to pieces, but my spirit still rejoices.

Second, when one takes a gander at scripture, you see time and time again how God created each one of us special, unique, and as a treasure for Him. As David writes in Psalm 139:13–15, "For it was you who formed my inward parts; you knit me together in my mother's womb. I praise you because I am fearfully and wonderfully made … My frame was not hidden from you, when I was being made in secret, intricately woven in the depths of the earth" (NRSV).

Minister and author, Ricky Macklin wrote *God Doesn't Make Junk* (2011). Even if you feel like rubbish—or the world sees you as inconsequential debris—God prizes you without parallel. His love and affection for you knows no bounds simply because He made you just as you are! Each one of us is truly one of a kind.

Finally, God the Father loves you because He sent His Son to die in your place so you can live eternally. It is an immutable truth that everyone has to die one death. Yet, Lord Jesus stood in the gap and died on the cross. He took all our wrongdoings away from all of us so that we could be made perfect and without blemish, allowing us as forgiven believers to eternally be with Father God in heaven—regardless of what we have done on earth. So beautiful. Now that is God's love!

ENJOY THE GO!

There is an American television commercial that sports jubilant animated bears in bathrooms using toilet tissue with the moniker, "Enjoy the Go!"[14] The implication is campy, but the notion is that by using their bath tissue, what would normally be unpleasant or uncomfortable is now fun or somehow satisfying. This commercial blurb is reminiscent of the opening verses of the book of James 2:3: "Consider it wholly joyful, my brethren, whenever you are enveloped in or encounter trials of any sort or fall into various temptations. Be assured and understand that the trial and proving of your faith bring out endurance and steadfastness and patience" (Amplified). Be wholly joyful? This is tough teaching, for it is hard and almost counterintuitive to imagine being delighted or elated during a difficult, onerous trial, tribulation, or a vexing temptation. Normally when things "hit the fan," we grit our teeth and slug our way out of a bad situation.

So, what is the thought process of having a "joy-filled" attitude when faced with adversity? Well, they say happiness comes from the spirit, but joy comes from the soul. Having said that, it seems that one's soul should not lose its luster during trying times. Saint Paul says in Philippians 4:4: "Rejoice in the Lord always" (NRSV). In 2 Corinthians 7:4: Paul writes, "I am overjoyed in all our afflictions" (NRSV). The underlying theme is that regardless of what is happening here on earth—in particular to our own lives—we *do* have a reserved place for us in the sky. Saint Paul continues in 2 Corinthians 6:10: "Your present suffering cannot compare to your future glory" (Amplified). Sounds good, but is this really comforting?

The problem here for us in the twenty-first century is that we live in

---

[14] Charmin by Procter & Gamble, Cincinnati, Ohio.

a me-me-me-now-now-now world where delayed gratification is not our strong suit. When James and Paul tell us to "Buck up!" during bad times and put a smile on our faces because better times are ahead in heaven, one almost thinks it sounds unrealistic or smacking of Pollyanna. Yet there is some logic as well as truth to this line of reasoning. If we are going through a difficult ordeal—if we embrace the situation with positive vim and vigor—then we have a much better chance of coming through it successfully. If you can do it with a great attitude—one with jubilance or alacrity—how much better or quicker will your prohibitive situation be resolved? Much more handily, I presume.

Moreover, one of the secrets to finding favor with the Lord is being thankful at all times. In the same way He hates and may prolong suffering for grumblers and murmurers (think of the Old Testament Israelites in the desert), He also is quick to bless those who remain strong and stout at heart during challenging times and through difficult ordeals. One can curry favor by always being thankful to God the Father for what His Son did for each one of us no matter what we go through at the moment on earth. Appreciation for the cross gladdens God the Father's heart every time.

It's not that every bump, bruise, or black eye should be taken with glee; that is masochism or self-flagellation. It is resolution of ordeal through good attitude, or simply put, the benefits of mind over matter. Making the best of a bad situation is usually the best way out of a bad situation!

ASK, PRAY, AND DEFER

In James 4:2: the scripture reads, "You do not have, because you do not ask" (ESV). It is a simple thing, but it is oh so important. Petitioning the Lord is threefold. You can pray for yourself. You can intercede and pray for others. Finally, you can pray with others. Regardless, when one prays, they should do so boldly with what is called "expectant faith," which is praying with full confidence and fervor that God will grant your petition or request. The hemorrhaging woman who touched Jesus's garment was healed because she believed so strongly it would be so. After she was healed, the Lord Jesus said to her (Matthew 5:22), "Daughter, your faith has made you well; go in peace, and be healed of your disease" (NRSV).

At the same time, as we pray for things we want, we also must recognize that God's will trumps everything. We saw in Exodus 30:14 (Moses on the mountain) that we can change God's mind through petition, but in general, if it ain't in His will, it ain't gonna happen. Full stop. His way or the highway. This truth can be particularly hard to swallow when we pray for healing (for ourselves and others), and it does not happen. We ask and do not receive. Then we have to acknowledge that God is truly sovereign, and His will be done even at the expense of the health and lives of people we love and care about. In short, we have to defer to God and what He wants. Full stop.

Years ago, a close relative had a CT scan, and the doctors found a tumor the size of an orange in her abdomen. My entire church and I prayed for God's intervention and healing. When the doctors went in to biopsy the tumor, it was miraculously gone. Chock one up for the good guys! Yet, when I broke my ankle, and it became infected, I had hundreds of people praying for me. Still, I lost my leg and my kidneys in the process. Yes, the Lord giveth, and the Lord also taketh away. Ouch!

Regardless of any outcome, we must earnestly ask, pray, and yes, in the end, defer to His will. All things will become known when we reach the heavenly places. We will understand why and how things turned out the way they did. Until then, we must trust Him and try, more than anything else, to see things from His eternal perspective. As it is written in Psalm 36:9: "[I]n your light, we see light" (NRSV). So must ask, pray, and ultimately defer. Amen.

John D. Emens, PhD

CURVEBALLS: PSALM 107

In the game of baseball and fast pitch softball, a good skillful pitcher has a bevy of different pitches they can throw at a batter: fastball, cut fastball, changeup, or a breaking ball, like a slider. Most pitchers have a money pitch, or best ball, like a fastball. Others throw the off-speed stuff or junk. A good fastball is hard to hit, but when connected, it is the easiest one to hit out of the park. Curveballs are breaking balls like sliders, but they have more velocity and rotate differently. In general, a good pitcher has good speed, location, and movement in throwing their pitches to strike out a batter.

The Lord is like a good pitcher. He likes to mix things up for us and sometimes keep us guessing, primarily for our benefit. The scriptures are chock-full of examples where the Lord throws a panoply of "curveballs" to His children for what seems to be a variety of reasons. In Psalm 107:4–5, God allows the Israelites who were lost or who "wander in desert wastes, finding no way to an inhabited town; hungry and thirsty" (Amplified). They called upon the Lord and were rescued ("he led them by a straight way, until they reached an inhabited town") (Psalm 107:7 NRSV).

In Psalm 107:10–11, God causes difficulty for us due to a rebellious attitude, which allows darkness and depression to occur to get people back on track: "Some sat in darkness and in the shadow of death, being bound in affliction and in irons because they had rebelled against the words of God, and spurned the counsel of the Most High" (Amplified). When they repented and sought the Lord, all was made better: "Then they cried to the Lord in their trouble and He saved them from their distress; He brought them out of darkness and gloom, and broke their bonds asunder" (Psalm 107:13–14 NRSV).

In Psalm 107:17–19, God afflicts people due to sin, and then He heals them when they cry for help: "Some are fools [made ill] because of the way of their transgressions and are afflicted of their iniquities. They loathe every kind of food, and they draw near to the gates of death. Then they cry to their Lord in their trouble, and He delivers them out of their distresses" (Amplified).

In Psalm 107:23–27 (NRSV), we see God testing us. He stirs up a storm on the great waters and puts people seemingly at risk: "Some went down to sea in ships … For He commanded and raised a stormy wind which lifted of the waves of the sea. They mounted up to the heaven, they went down to the depths; their courage melted away in their calamity; they reeled and staggered like drunkards, and were at wits end." Then after crying to the Lord, "He made the storm still and the waves hushed" (Psalm 107:29 NRSV).

You see, time and time again, God puts us in situations we cannot control just so He can be in control. He places us in what seems to be jeopardy just so we can be rescued by Him. Through this rescuing process, we learn to depend, trust, and rely on Him. We even learn to trust Him when it makes little sense just as in the book of Job where abject calamity befalls the protagonist. Job did nothing to bring upon himself the ill fortune that was brought upon him by the Lord. Must have been very confusing to Job.

In verse 42:11, the scripture reads that after the Lord restored Job's fortunes his family comforted him for "all the distressing calamites that the Lord had brought upon him [Job]" (Amplified). Another translation reads: "They showed him sympathy and comforted him for all the evil the Lord had brought upon him [Job]" (NRSV). In this book of the Bible, when Job recognized God's sovereignty or His right to throw disaster at him, God restored Job's fortunes by a factor of two. Job trusted God despite calamity, and the Lord richly rewarded him for doing so.

Finally, God seems to allow all of us to go through a "boot camp" where we struggle and are refined to be more what He intends us to be. As it reads in 1 Peter 5:10–11, where he tells us to be "steadfast in your faith, for you know that your brothers and sisters in all the world are undergoing the same kind of suffering. And after you have suffered for a little while, the God of all grace, who has called you to His eternal glory in Christ, will himself restore, support, strengthen, and establish you" (NRSV). Sounds a bit like the US military where they "tear you down to build you up."

So, God does throw curveballs, mostly for our own good. Sometimes the curveballs make sense, and sometimes they don't. But by trusting in Him and acknowledging His sovereignty, we move forward and are then most likely, as in baseball, to "connect" and get a "hit." Some might resent His intervening, but one should always remember what it says in Proverbs 3:12: "For whom the Lord loveth he corrects; even as a father the son in whom he delights" (KJV). God is a person, and He loves us. He will be with us in times of trouble, but we should also recognize He will do His best to keep us from drifting away. Hence, curveballs come our way to keep us on the straight and narrow. Amen.

WHERE ANGELS FEAR TO TREAD: SOLOMON'S RULE

There is an old saying that one should not go where "angels fear to tread." This quotation is not from scripture; instead, it is a derivation of a line from Thomas Hardy. In 1887, he penned, "Fools rush in where angels fear to tread." The meaning is clear, namely, that one should be careful where one goes or travels because some places are more dangerous than others.

In Proverbs 5:7–8, Solomon warns, "And now, my child, listen to me, and do not depart from the words of my mouth. Keep your way far from her [the harlot], and do not go near the door of her house" (NRSV). Even Jesus chose to avoid going to Judea at one time just to avoid being killed by the Jewish Pharisees. In John 7:1, the scripture reads: "After this Jesus went from place to place in Galilee. He did not go to Judea because the Jews were looking for an opportunity to kill Him" (NRSV). Even Christ watched his own steps carefully. The upshot is what I would call Solomon's Rule: namely, that one should not put themselves in a position where one might make a poor decision or place themselves directly in harm's way. Avoid the street corners where the prostitutes roam. Paul warns that drunkards and gluttons will not see the kingdom of God; the implication is not to hang around such persons or practice such oneself.

On the other hand, Jesus was known to eat and drink with tax collectors, prostitutes, and other "sinners," but we need to remember He is the Lord and has perfect self-control. Being in proximity to unhelpful influences is reminiscent of the previously mentioned idea of neutrality. For Jesus, being around drunkards who need help or the sick who need a doctor, to Him, is not "dangerous" or an onerous source of temptation. In many ways, it all depends on the person. I used to be a drinker, but it no longer has any appeal for me. I can go into a liquor store and buy some bubble gum and have no problem, but can a non-recovering alcoholic? Proximity matters to those to whom influences are not neutral. Recall Solomon's Rule. Do you really want your ten year-old kid to see an R- or X-rated movie?

In 1985, I was to take a job with a Wall Street investment banking firm. A fortnight after I accepted the job offer, I had a powerful encounter with the Holy Spirit that changed my life. After careful consideration, I decided to turn down the banking job, sensing I wasn't yet strong enough in my faith to "run with the bulls on Wall Street." True, God needs believers everywhere, but I felt it wasn't my time. I deferred to the Spirit and continued with my graduate work and eventually went into teaching. Again, Solomon's Rule.

They say believers are to be *in* the world but not *of* the world. Proximity matters for those whose inclinations are not neutral. It seems that where an angel should fear to tread depends as much on the angel as it does on where they tread. God made us all angels, but He didn't make us all godly. Amen.

ENJOYING THE BATTLE

One night, in the early days of my Christian walk, I had a long conversation with an elder of our church. He started recounting the early days of our congregation and how taxing they were on him, for he was a super-busy person who "wore all hats." He had administrative responsibilities and was extensively organizing and managing the youth groups. He also was involved in managing the evangelism teams. To put even more pressure on him, he held an important government job in the State Department. After a number of years doing all these different duties, his energy wore thin. He became fatigued and emotionally drained. At one point, he didn't know how long he could keep it up. He was ready to give up.

My elder friend then told me that one night, in exhaustion, he prayed fervently to God, "O Lord Jesus, I don't know how long I can keep all this up. I am so weary and becoming at a loose end. How long must I keep at all these roles in the church? I am not so sure I can." My friend looked me in the eye and said, "Jack, in my spirit, I sensed the Lord intuited to me that it was time I started enjoying the battle." Reenergized and inspired, my elder friend was then able to redouble his efforts and continue working for the church with a refreshed attitude and a gladdened heart.

The key phrase here is "enjoying the battle." We need to remember that even though we are in an onerous struggle between good and evil in our modern, contemporary fallen world—with all its faults and foibles, ups and downs, and triumphs and tragedies—we still should enjoy and relish the opportunity to serve our Most High God. With eagerness and stout hearts, we must soldier on! Amen!

John D. Emens, PhD

HELPFUL AMNESIA

Forgiveness. It's hard sometimes, but it's not as hard as forgetting. When people do us wrong, it is hard to let go and "forgive and forget." We want justice. Yet, many times, when people hurt us, they do not come forth with contrition and say they are sorry. Without an apology, it is sometimes hard to pardon. But forgiving even without the apology is a good thing; it releases us of the bitter hurt and the emotional wound. Forgiveness from the heart is a healthy, healing choice that makes a victim into a victor. Forgiveness may be a first step to eliminating shame if the hurt is severe. Put the incident behind you. Think of it as helpful amnesia. Blot out the injury. Let the consequences fall on them. Be free! Free indeed. Amen.

GIFTED PEOPLE

Some people are smarter than others. Some people are more athletic than others. Some people just know how to turn a buck, and others, like my wife, have good finger dexterity and can quilt, knit, and crochet. Some have excellent people skills, and others can barely shake hands. Some are good speakers, articulate and eloquent; others wouldn't be caught dead orating from a podium in front of other folk. Some have photographic memories; others can't remember their own phone numbers, especially now that we have cell phones. As Paul writes in 1 Corinthians 12:27: "Now you [collectively] are Christ's body and [individually] you are members of it, each part severally and distinct [each with its own place and function]" (Amplified).

Yet having many gifts does not say it all. Being able to perform well at any task or undertaking also takes heart, pluck, and character; these three are the requisite gasolines that make the glorious Christian life run. Being stout at heart with nerve, courage, mettle, and integrity motivates the gifts and makes us more useful. Having a gift is one thing, but being able to use it and use it well is another.

Finally, there is one kind of gift not yet mentioned, and that is the ability to care, love, and show charity to others; this is the greatest gift. Again, as Paul writes in 1 Corinthians 12:31: "But earnestly desire the highest gifts and graces (the higher gifts and choicest graces). And yet I will show you a still more excellent way [one that is better by far and the highest of them all—love]" (Amplified).

John D. Emens, PhD

THE INSECURE BULLY

Bullies are big and demonstrably loud, but they are also very weak. Driven by personal insecurities and emotional handicaps, they may wreak havoc on the meek and mild. Bullies take pleasure in other people's pain, primarily because they somehow have a need for it. Bullies are everywhere, be it biggest kid on the playground to the pestilent doctor who lords it over his or her nurses or assistants, the unsuccessful investment banker who kicks around his underling associates on Wall Street, or the unpopular professor who likes to flunk most the class. All these bullies find devilish joy in other people's misery; they are suffering a disease, a malady of temperament. Truly, they are the ones who are the exceptionally needy. We avoid bullies like the plague, which is another reason why they browbeat and torment others. They want to be noticed. For some bullies, if they cannot get good attention, they settle for bad attention.

Bullies are to be pitied. In their pathetic attempts to be big shots by compromising others, they make complete, unambiguous fools of themselves. Deep inside, bullies are lonely emotional weaklings, thinking that by eclipsing other folks' esteem, they will somehow augment theirs. Reprehensible and noxious as they are, bullies are to be seen with compassion since they are in fact actually quite timid, confused, and emotionally frail. Although they show bombast and bluster to impress, what they really need is a good and sincere friend. They need love and someone to trust. They crave affirmation and unconditional acceptance (like all of us, really).

Sometimes we need to take courage, put down our pride, and pick up our cross. Loving the unlovable or unloved is a virtue. It is not easy, but it is ardently crown-worthy.

Ruby-Throated Hummingbird

The ruby-throated hummingbird has black wings, a gray speckled undercarriage, and a bright crimson gullet area. Territorial in their feeding areas, they live on plant nectar or small insects. Their wings beat fast, and so do their hearts—more than a thousand beats per minute. They have the highest metabolism of any fowl, and they migrate hundreds of miles a year. They get their name—hummingbird—from the light buzzing sound their supersonic beating wings make. Their life span is relatively short, and their small size makes them prey from ground-dwelling reptiles to other larger birds of the air. Almost asexual, they mate for only a moment, and they do not develop long-term relationships with their partners.

Upon observation, the hummingbirds I have witnessed seemed frenetic, frenzied, and almost wigged out. Aesthetically beautiful to the eye, pleasant to the ear, and a marvel to behold, hummingbirds are patently unique—and spotting them is a rare treat. Seeing them prance and dance around a bright red nectar birdfeeder or flit from flower to flower is an amazing spectacle. Like a glistening, shimmering sunset or the bright pulsating canvas of the night Milky Way, spying a hummingbird shows a snapshot of God's creation at work. Buzzing wings are poetry in motion, and their bright colors are like bright sparks flying out from a crackling, spuming summer campfire.

Hummingbirds. Now you seem 'em; now you don't. Kind of like us—the quick and the dead.

John D. Emens, PhD

ANGER, RESENTMENT, AND HATE

We all get angry at times. When we are truly wronged or emotionally compromised it is understandable that we experience umbrage and indignation. If not dealt with in a practical, favorable way, it turns into resentment. Over time, resentment not abated can turn into hate. Hate eats away at us to our core, burns up our energy, wounds our esteem, and in general, is just bad karma. So, if anger is the original motivator of all these unhelpful proclivities, how do we handle it? How do we operationalize anger in a way that does not bring us down? What do we do when we are stinkin' hopping mad? Good question.

Ephesians 4:26 reads, "Be angry and do not sin" (ESV). First Peter 3:9 says, "Do not repay evil for evil or insult with insult" (NIV). Yet, we all have feelings, and sometimes when we get hurt, we want vengeance or payback. The Bible is clear that we need to trust God to judge those who hurt us. In Romans 12:19, it reads, "Beloved, never avenge yourselves, but leave room for the wrath of God; for it is written, 'Vengeance is mine, I will repay, says the Lord'" (ESV). In fact, in Proverbs 25:21–22, it says to be good to people who harm or injure us. "If thine enemy be hungry, give him bread to eat; and if he be thirsty, give him water to drink: For thou shalt heap coals of fire upon his head and the Lord shall reward thee" (KJV). Romans 12:21 also says, "Be not overcome with evil, but overcome evil with good" (NIV).

In short, we need faith, patience, compassion, and pity. We need faith that God will take vengeance for us and that He will reward us if we are good to those who compromise us. Second, we need patience to let this all play out—to leave room for grace and let God work in the situation.

Third, we need compassion to perhaps have understanding for the persons who harm or wrong us; if we try to understand why someone transgresses upon us, it may abate or lessen the fervor or burn of our anger; it may help reduce the resentment that fuels hate and enmity. Finally, we can even pity the person who trespasses against us, and in doing so, we can walk away as the emotionally stronger party. We are now the victor—not the victim.

Anger is understandable, but it can be dangerous. At times, we need to just do our level best to put our feelings aside—even simply for our own good and well-being. As it says in Proverbs 29:22: "One given to anger stirs up strife, and the hothead causes much transgression" (NRSV).

DIAMOND DOGS

The scriptures put a premium on believers practicing their faith with persistence, endurance, and perseverance. The RSV translation of Hebrews 12:1 says, "Let us run with perseverance the race set before us." The Amplified translation of the same verse reads: "Let us run the race with patient endurance and steady active persistence the appointed course of the race set before us." To be brief, the Christian walk is a marathon and not a sprint. Dogged diligence and stick-to-itiveness are essential—and it may not be easy or painless—to reap the end rewards we so desire. As it says in Revelation 2:10: "Do not fear what you have to suffer ... Be faithful to the end and I will give you the crown of life" (NRSV).

Truth be known, persistence, endurance, and perseverance are learned or acquired attributes and not necessarily gifts from above. How does one obtain these qualities? The short answer is by unrelenting effort over time and trial and error. Nineteenth-century author and reformer Samuel Smiles once said, "The best sort of character, however, cannot be formed without effort." Do not be afraid to fail or make mistakes. Novelist Joseph Conrad once wrote, "It's only those who do nothing that make no mistakes." No bones about it, with rigor and vigor, dividends are reaped. Second Chronicles 15:7 reads: "Be ye strong therefore, and let not your hands be weak; for your work will be rewarded" (KJV).

Developing these qualities and attributes is part and parcel of the ongoing refining process in the Christian walk. Usually, these qualities are acquired by facing challenges and overcoming difficulties. As it says in Isaiah 48:10: "See, I have refined you, but not like silver; I have tested you in the furnace of adversity" (NRSV). To be pithy and didactic: no pain, no gain.

As we learn, grow, work, and develop these enduring qualities, we become more useful, proficient, and productive, and we also become rare gems ourselves. As my high school swimming coach used to say, "A diamond is a lump of coal that hung in there a little longer." We become the product through the process itself. As Paul writes in Philippians 1:6 :"He who began a good work in you will continue until the day of Jesus Christ [right up until the time of His return] developing [that good work] and perfecting and bringing it to full completion in you" (Amplified). Amen. So be it!

ROMPER ROOM GODLY SERVICE

I have been wrong about many things over the years, but one area in which I have been consistently misguided has been in my attitude toward service for the Lord. For many years, I served the Lord because I wanted to please Him—but not for the right reasons. As a young Christian, I sought to serve the Lord and others not only because I wanted to please Him but also because I thought it was the best way to actually get the things I wanted for myself. I thought if I did all the right things—prayed, read the Bible, went to church, put beaucoup bread in the plate, and performed good deeds— that God would be more likely to reward me. I worked for the Lord to seek His favor and gifts. Well, that kind of infantile theology would be good for *Romper Room* (a TV show for toddlers), but it doesn't fly when you grow up, really get to know the Lord, and appreciate all He has done and will do for you.

God through Christ offers eternal life. As it says in 2 Timothy 1:10: "But it is now made manifest by the appearing of our Savior Jesus Christ, who hath abolished death, and hath brought to life and immortality to light through the gospel" (KJV). First John 5:11 reads, "And this is the record, that God hath given to us eternal life, and this life is in his Son" (KJV). In John 14:2–3, Jesus says, "In My Father's house there are many dwelling places (homes). If it were not so, I would have told you: for I am going away to prepare a place for you. And when (if) I go and make ready a place for you, I will come back again to take you to Myself, that where I am you may be also." [Amplified]. Yes, it is clear a rich life awaits us on the other side.

As I began to really understand what Christ's sacrifice and death meant and how it covered all past, present, and future wrongs—as well as punching my ticket to heaven—I began to serve out of sheer thankfulness and gratefulness. In life in general, when someone does something nice for you—buys you lunch or mows your lawn—you want to give something back to them. You are thankful and grateful, and you want to reciprocate. Gift for gift. The same is true with the Lord when one is a mature Christian. When you really know the real value of God's gift of salvation, you want to serve out of a grateful and thankful mind and heart. It is that simple.

When I now serve the Lord, I expect nothing back. He has already given me my gift. Every little deed I do is like a simple thank-you note to the Lord in the mail. How He may or may not choose to bless me back is totally up to Him. All I am trying to do is take a lesson from Him in unconditional love. He loves me no matter what—so, why should I serve Him with motives of subterfuge and trying to bless Him to get what I want? Although I am, as we all are, a work in progress, through time, He has taught me how to serve Him, as the Israelites did in 2 Chronicles 7:10: "Joyful and glad in heart for the good things the Lord had done" (NIV).

Ignatius of Loyola (1491–1556) said, "God will not be outdone in generosity." We should take note of this and try to thankfully and gratefully beat Him at His own game.

John D. Emens, PhD

DEPRESS-SHUN

When I was sixteen years old, my uncle David and I were trying out a new outboard motorboat for possible purchase on Glen Lake, near Glen Arbor, Michigan. It was an incredibly capricious windy day, and the waves on the lake were large and unpredictable. We drove the sixteen-foot runabout downwind to the far end of the lake. Going with the waves was easy, but as we motored farther along, we realized that going back to the marina where we launched the boat might be a real challenge. The waves were about five feet, which was large for a small lake, and making it back was going to be difficult and perhaps dangerous. Yet, with little choice, we turned the small craft around and headed directly into the waves at a slow but steady speed. The only way to keep the boat from tipping over was to hit the waves smack-dab head-on. We carefully chugged up the lake at reduced speed with the waves, spray, and spume crashing over the bow. Directly into the wind, the farther back we motored, the smaller the waves became. Eventually, when we were in calm enough waters, we opened her up until we reached the small marina at the other end of the lake; once there, we safely moored the boat. We made it! Whew!

In life, you sometimes have to also hit your challenges head-on. This is true in the physical, mental, and emotional realms. Right now, at present, I am dealing with physical maladies; I am on dialysis and learning to walk on a prosthesis. In my younger days, however, I went through a serious, prolonged bout with depression. I suffered some serious wrongs in my youth, and coupled with the breakup with my first wife, I was thrown into a deep pit of darkness, despair, and despondency. For many years, I had ignored dealing with the issues that troubled me, and at the age of forty, it all caught up with me. I couldn't work or do much of anything else for more than a year. Finally, I got help and got down to the business of why I was feeling so melancholy. I was out of touch with my feelings, and I had shunned dealing with the causes of my deep pain. When I faced my emotional demons directly and dealt with the deep anger and hurt, I eventually got better. Slow but steady progress. In the end, when I able to truly forgive those who had aggrieved me, I came out of my depression completely. Joy and peace bubbled to the surface; now healed, my test became my testimony. And as I have since helped others in similar situations, there ended up being purpose to my pain.

What is the lesson here? Sometimes, the last thing we want to do is exactly what we should do. Hard choices require courage at times. The last thing I wanted to do was to take off my leg, yet it was infected to the bone, and as I was and am now seeking a kidney transplant, I had to amputate since one cannot get a transplant with any infection. The same is true in the mental, emotional, and spiritual realms. Rest assured, not dealing with root causes of any malady—shunning the problem—just prolongs and can even exacerbate the problem. Directly identifying the concern, and dealing with it, is the best way to overcome it. Just like in radiating and eradicating a cancerous tumor, one must specify and pinpoint any problem to subdue and eventually conquer it.

In these troublesome situations, like with the motorboat on Glen Lake, going directly into and against the oncoming waves, is the best thing to do. Ignoring the problem and continuing to ride with the waves just floats you up a creek without a paddle.

John D. Emens, PhD

G-R-A-C-E

The other day, I heard a remark at a church event that puzzled me. Some friends were speaking about being heavily anointed and richly blessed. The comment was that the service "had a lot of grace!"

I said, "What's a lot of grace? Everything is grace."

They shook their heads and didn't know how to reply.

We then began a long discussion on the meaning of grace, which is a critical and central tenet of the Christian faith and in particular, the New Testament.

Grace, by definition, means "unmerited favor by God." You cannot earn grace or favor. It is a free gift, and one can only receive it. There are some things in life we cannot control or initiate: the weather, the ozone, or the price of gas for that matter (for the most part). The same is true for favor from the Lord; you can only accept what He offers. Where the confusion arose with my friends in our aforementioned discussion was the difference between grace, blessing, and anointment. When they had a powerful prayer meeting, they said the meeting had "a lot of grace." Truth be known, any meeting has grace. In fact, everything created in this universe is grace. A well-known old acronym for grace is "God's riches at Christ's expense." The point is that everything created is God's riches, from the food we eat, to the air we breathe, to the orbit of our planet earth around the sun.

What my friends meant to say was that the meeting was powerfully anointed or richly blessed. Anointed, by definition, means "rubbing with oil," in a physical sense, but to be sanctified or "set apart" by the action of the Holy Spirit in a spiritual sense. Blessings are a direct function of God's given generosity within a covenant consanguinity, or affiliation, with believers. To say a meeting is "full of grace" is a non sequitur; it's like saying that a forward pass is full of football or that a monkey wrench has lots of tool in it. These statements are undeniably true, and descriptive, but they are not particularly useful, helpful, or explanatory.

Saint John uses the term "full of grace and truth"[15] to describe Jesus Christ, but the Lord has the Spirit "without limit," according to the scriptures. "Without limit" is just another way of saying infinite, which is exactly what grace is: infinite, ubiquitous, omnipresent. In a word, it is universal.

Is this discussion nitpicky? Maybe, but at the end of the day, through this dialogue, we can recognize that He made everything; therefore, we owe everything to the One and Only. Understanding this universal paradigm is just one more reason to be unabashedly humble and unapologetically grateful in our hearts to our marvelous Creator. Amen.

---

[15] John 1:14 (NIV).

DIRTY DIAPERS

Years ago, I heard a talk where someone remarked that when we make a wrong or commit a sin, it is like a bad odor to God. In a sense, we become smelly until we repent and ask for forgiveness. Having done so, we are once again in a good and right relationship with the Lord. Now we smell just fine; yes, we got our diaper change.

The "diaper change" metaphor is particularly apt on a number of levels. First, with an infant, frequent diaper changes are understandable and expected; the bad "smells" are just part and parcel of the program. Similarly, new Christians or unbelievers may have a lot of "baggage;" they may be benignly hip deep in dirty diapers; this is also to be expected.

It is hard to blame a newborn for what is recognized to be a natural function or a universally acceptable behavior for their age. The same is true for a non-Christian; it is understandable to err when one doesn't yet know the typical parameters or norms of right or wrong in the first place. When non-Christians commit or unknowingly fall into wrongs or offenses, God is incredibly patient, hoping to get them first into the corral and commencing with diaper changes shortly thereafter. Newborns always get the most tender and patient care of all.

Second, like most folks, after time passes, a toddler grows up and dispenses of his or her need for typical diapers. Now in regular clothes, the child has bad "smells" far less frequently. And, even though the more mature Christian is more able to better control his or her thoughts and actions, "accidents," or sin, can still and will happen; this too is to be expected. When this happens to all of us, we repent with contrition, and the "smelliness" is eliminated once again. Such is the evolution of a natural Christian walk.

Third, there are the immature Christians who seem to never get out of their diapers; they seem to carry bad "smells" with them much more of the time than would be the norm. If these are relatively innocuous trespasses, the dirty diapers may be somewhat negotiable between the person and God. Diaper changes may continue until God can have His way. I smoked for more than a decade as a young Christian before the Lord asked me to quit (and I did—that day, actually). If there are more serious dirtying of diapers that involve longer-term consequences for others, then "adults" may have to get involved in cleaning up such behaviors, from gentle nudges or suggestions to tough love, to interventions (to maybe even blowing the whistle for the authorities). As we all know, dirty diapers on adults are treated differently than those on young folk—as are the penalties. Gentle He is to a point, but firm, depending on the person and provocation.

Fourth, no matter how strong and mature a Christian becomes, there are some diaper "smells" that may creep upon us. They may not be of the typical physical variety, but of the mind and spirit, and the most dangerous one is pride. The more one knows, the more wisdom one acquires. The more one seems to have it all together, the more likely one is to fall into the trap of ego aggrandizement or overactive pride.

Pride, one of the seven deadly sins," is particularly "smelly" to the Lord, and it is a true pitfall for believers. In James 4:6, Lord says, "God opposes the proud, but gives grace to the humble" (ESV). Unchecked arrogance seems to be in vogue in our contemporary society, and everyone has been taught to "look out for number one." However, the Lord wants to be "tooting the horn," not us, and He eventually gets around to letting us know that truth—kindly or not so kindly.

Finally, there are some people who never seem to "get it." They consistently and unapologetically dirty their diapers for their entire lives. On earth, we put these folks in homes or penal institutions, depending on culpability. As for them in the afterlife? Well, that one is up to Lord Jesus, and He thankfully is in the mercy seat. Amen.

John D. Emens, PhD

THE GOLDFINCH

Today, outside the Dollar General store, I spied a delightful tiny goldfinch resting on a cattail by a water culvert on the side of Delaware Avenue. The bird was bright yellow in breast and wing and dappled with noir near the wingtips. Head brisk and perky with his maize face cloaked with a Batman-looking black mask. Dark eyes darting back and forth, my little winged friend was partially hidden in the high green foliage, weaving to and fro in the softly gusting breeze.

Whenever I see a goldfinch, which isn't often, I think of my grandfather. Goldfinches were Popper's favorite bird. When I was seven or eight years old, I made a painted plastic model of a goldfinch out of a hobby kit. I gave it to Popper for his birthday, and he was tickled pink. He was so pleased. Making my grandfather happy made me happy. I beamed with pride and satisfaction.

I sorely miss my grandfather, although it has been forty years since he passed. He was of a rare breed of high ambition, keen smarts, beaucoup wisdom, genuine humility, and gentle kindness. He was taciturn without being aloof or antisocial, and he nearly always sported an insufferable positive attitude that was coupled with measured seriousness that came from a life of hard work. He truly enjoyed people, and he was quick with a firm handshake and a nod of the head. He enjoyed a good joke or quick quip, and he was fond of telling stories of his days on the family farm from his youth. He had entrepreneurial vision and good practical business sense. Even though a believer, he rarely ever talked religion, and never once did I hear Popper criticize anyone in public office. He oozed integrity, and one of his pet peeves was people who exaggerated and used inexactitudes in speech and action. He was incisive and decisive, promptly telling my grandmother he would marry her on their very first date. Athletic, he water-skied at the age of sixty, and he was my personal golf instructor when I started the game at age six. Extremely demanding of himself, but forgiving and understanding with others, Popper was a most uncommon and remarkable person; I was lucky to have him for sixteen years.

So, I sit in my Honda Civic with the window rolled down as I wait for my wife to finish shopping. I glance back out toward the rusted gray culvert, and I see the goldfinch has vanished. I promptly close my eyes for a final thought about Popper, and I smile, especially because I know right now, in this moment, my grandfather is watching me from above.

John D. Emens, PhD

HOLY SWIPE

One summer during my college years, a friend from a well-to-do family invited me out to New York City for a weeklong vacay. Her family lived outside of the city, but they also had a place on the Upper East Side. As a wet-behind-the-ears Midwesterner from Ohio, I felt a little out of sorts having never been to the Big Apple—and I didn't have the coin to make the trip. I talked things over with my father, and he always encouraged me to embrace new experiences. When I said I didn't have the cash for the weeklong holiday, he smiled, pulled out his personal credit card, and told me to have a week "on him." Thanks, Dad!

Like William Wordsworth, who penned, "When ... I lie in vacant or pensive mood,"[16] I too sometimes muse or daydream. For Wordsworth, it was about daffodils. For me, it is about how Jesus actually wipes away my wrongdoings. How does He actually "pay" for my sins? I know when I die, I will have to face my Lord sitting on the judgment seat. I know that I will have to answer for my sins on earth. In my dream, I confess my foibles, mistakes, and wrongdoings. Then I smile, think of my father and the New York trip, and similarly imagine Jesus handing me a holy credit card, and hopefully saying, "Well done, good and faithful servant.[17] Just swipe here—your sins are on me. Zero balance. Welcome to heaven. Tours begin soon to see the Father. Why don't we now just sit down and spend some quality time together. I have been looking forward to seeing you for quite some time. We have so much to share."

---

[16] William Wordsworth, "I Wandered Lonely as Cloud," published in "Poems in Two Volumes" (1807).
[17] Matthew 25:21 (NIV).

I have little doubt that there is no such a thing as a heavenly, sin-covering, "holy swipe" credit card. However, my faith is all but certain that when I meet Him face-to-face, there will be a good chance I will find myself debt free. Thanks be to God!

POWER OF THE PURSE

My wife has a purse the size of Yankee Stadium. In it, she has nearly everything under the sun: chewing gum, hand sanitizer, my sunglass clip-ons, nail clippers and file, ChapStick, candy bar (for diabetic emergencies), handkerchief, extra prosthesis socks, small flashlight, spare keys, and wallet with money and plastic enclosed. Although a royal pain to lug around, her large purse has something for just about any situation. Whatever I need, I can just freely pull out of her handbag (and I do).

I liken the purse to how I think about the importance of reading and knowing the scriptures. The Bible is not simply about God; it is about the character and personality of God. Through the scriptures, I don't just believe in God; through them, I know Him and how He has acted and reacted in a zillion situations. Like my wife's handbag, or purse, whatever situation I am in, or train of thought I am running, if I need to, by knowing the Bible I, can usually pull out a ready scripture to give me guidance. This is a valuable asset for myself and for helping others. The Bible is my toolbox, and the more tools I have—the more scriptures I am familiar with—the more I can effectively apply them.

Moreover, when I am deep in fervent prayer and am listening intently for that still small voice of the Lord, all He has to do is say a word or two, and I know where to go in the Bible to follow up. Psalm 119:105 reads: "Your word is a lamp to my feet and a light to my path" (NRSV). Knowing well the scriptures gives me a floodlight for almost any situation—a ready reference guide for life. This helps me, and it makes me more useful and valuable to the Lord to help others.

Some people think the Bible is passé or arcane. Funny, it has been the all-time best seller across the world for centuries—even now. Yet, sadly enough, the Holy Word has never made it on the *New York Times* Bestseller's List.

HOLY ONES FIRST

This past week, I lost my close friend Michael to cancer. It has been of late a very emotionally trying time. In this past month, my wife and I have also lost four other members of our church. I look at the world with the pandemic and all the bad weather, earthquakes, flooding, famine, disease, gun violence, terrorism, and war, and I ponder if we truly are in Revelation's end-times. All the signs are there, but such a question is beyond my expertise to ascertain. I just have to trust God and know that He is in charge, and no matter what happens, there is no panic in heaven. I know none of these things catch God off guard, for He is all-knowing.

Yet I have to wonder: Why Michael? Why now? And why are others who are so special to me dying now? If I were to hazard a guess, I would have to say God is taking His holy ones first.

PEACE = F (TRUST)

My wife makes good chili; she makes it the variety that everybody loves. I make spicy chili—the kind most people gag over. To make my fiery concoction so insanely flammable, my recipe calls for Spicy V-8, chopped jalapeno peppers, black ground pepper, chopped green peppers, onion, and finally, gobs of chili powder. In a sense—and in a mathematical gibberish—my chili spiciness is a function of those six ingredients.

Similarly, in the Christian faith, peace or tranquility is a function of many things. At the outset, one must recognize the key ingredient being the presence of the Holy Spirit, which as it says in Philippians 4:7 gives us the "peace which passeth all understanding" (KJV). Christ himself said in John 14:27: "Peace I leave with you; my peace I give to you. I do not give to you as the world gives. Do not let your hearts be troubled, and do not be afraid" (NIV).

Ostensibly, there is lots in the world we could be troubled and fearful about. What is the most potent antidote to this "fear" or trepidation in the world around us? Trusting in God. Peace is a direct function of trust, the single most important ingredient in the recipe for tranquility—no matter what deleterious events might come down the pipe. The higher the level of trust, the more pronounced the level of peace. It is arguably that simple.

Trust doesn't come easily; a lot may depend somewhat on our upbringing and how life may have treated us. Yet, with the Lord, if we can openly accept His faithfulness with the trust of a child, we may find fear and anxiety abate remarkably regardless of any prevailing bad circumstance. As it says in Isaiah 26:3–4: "Those of steadfast mind you keep in peace—in peace they trust in you. Trust in the Lord forever, for in the Lord God you have an everlasting rock" (NRSV).

How to trust? Trust like a child? It's hard, but it is helpful to know

John D. Emens, PhD

that trust is the opposite side of the coin of faith. Faith, in Hebrews 11:1 is defined as "the substance of things hoped for, the evidence of things not seen (KJV)." The New American Standard translation refers to "the conviction of things not seen." At some point, faith takes conviction or courage. We have all heard the phrase "leap of faith." There is also a "leap of trust;" it too takes conviction and courage. This courage may take an extra amount of bravery if you have been burned a bit in life or come from the "school of hard knocks." Furthermore, as any good psychologist might observe, trusting your Father in heaven might be more difficult if your own dad in life wasn't good to you. They say that many times, we naturally picture our Father God in heaven as we have known and feel about our paternal parent here on earth.

Regardless, in the final analysis, we need to know—more than anything else—that we can trust in Him. He truly cares for us. As it says in 1 Peter 5:8: "Casting the whole of your care [all your anxieties, worries, all your concerns, once and for all] on Him, for He cares about you watchfully" (Amplified). Yes, we must avoid worry because it is the true symptom of a lack of trust. Just as this last passage from 1 Peter indicates, by casting our care or worries onto Him, we are throwing our problems and situations in His court, and we are trusting in Him that He will bring our trials to pass. Remember, He sees it all—the big picture—from start to finish. He can steer us through any rough seas or choppy waters.

Finally, in the parable of the sower in Matthew 13:22, the "cares of the world" are part of the "distractions" that "choke" the Word so it "yields no fruit" [Amplified]. By worrying and not trusting, we hurt ourselves, and we also render ourselves useless. Let us look to Him, trust in Him, and let the chips fall as they may. In the final analysis, we know that "all things work for good for those who love God and called according to his purpose" (Romans 8:28 NRSV). Amen.

My Way or Yahweh

We live in a very busy, egocentric world. At times, it is very hard to obey God; this too seems to be true for many individuals in the Bible. The scriptures are chock-full of examples of folks who were or were not obedient. Jonah did all he could to avoid and evade God's call and claim on his life. In the end, Jonah submitted to God's will, and he did what the Lord asked—although after going through due duress for nearly an entire book of the Bible.

On the other hand, Abraham was obedient (except for Ishmael) to the fullest, placing his own son Isaac on the sacrificial altar as God so commanded him. In doing so, Abraham became the "father of many nations."[18] Noah's obedience to God salvaged his life and the lives of his family. Daniel openly obediently prayed to the Lord against the decree of King Darius. Mary was unhesitant in obediently submitting to God's will in carrying the child Jesus when first asked by the archangel Gabriel. Jesus Himself was obedient unto death: "He poured out himself to death, and was numbered with the transgressors, yet he bore the sins of many, and made intercession for the transgressors" (Isaiah 53:12 NRSV). John the Baptist was obedient, he but lost his head over preaching a Gospel of repentance (literally). Peter, whose pure disobedience, or desertion of the Lord, was forgiven, eventually became the genesis or founder of the Christian Church in Jerusalem. Paul, an outright persecutor of the Christian Church, like Christ, became obedient unto death in Rome after preaching the Gospel worldwide.

God rewards obedience, but how do we become so? He teaches us obedience if we listen and learn. When we first come to know Him, we

---

[18] Genesis 17:4 (NIV).

do so by His answering our prayer of salvation. Afterward, He begins to work in us and in our hearts and minds to become more like Him—more kind, loving, and patient. In doing so, we develop the "fruit of the spirit."[19] We learn by listening to the Holy Spirit as He dwells in us, comforts us, counsels us, and consoles us. When disobedient, we grieve the Spirit, and only by repenting and coming back into His will do we restore peace and right relationship. If we are totally off track, we may lose what is called "unrestrained grace," and life may get way out of sorts until we come around to being in His will. In Proverbs 3:2 it reads, "My child, do not despise the Lord's discipline or be weary of his reproof, for the Lord reproves the one he loves, as a father the son in whom he delights" (NRSV).

Perhaps the hardest part of obedience is learning to take things in His way and in His time. Patience is hard, but as it says in Hebrews 10:36, "For ye have need of patience, that after ye have done the will of God, ye might receive the promise" (KJV). His timing is perfect, but waiting can be hard. Patience is earned. We live in a "me-first" fast-food contemporary world, and we have to learn to abide and patiently wait on Him. In doing so, we please Him and are more useful to Him. As it says in 1 Samuel 15:22: "Has the Lord as great delight in burnt offerings and sacrifices, as in obedience to the voice of the Lord? Surely, to obey is better than sacrifice, and to heed than the fat of rams" (NRSV). In other words, directly following God's will in heartfelt obedience is better than doings things we think He may want, such as the knee-jerk sacrifices that so many seemed to perform in the Old Testament.

This discussion begs the question of how we know God's will. We do this by knowing, understanding, and listening. We generally know we are on the right track by how the Spirit resides in us. When we are abiding, it says in Philippians 4:7 that the Spirit gives us the "peace the passeth all understanding" (KJV). If we are off track, we may lose some measure of that peace. Secondly, we glean understanding by familiarity with the scriptures that give guidance.

Finally, we can listen in deep prayer for the still small voice of the Lord, which although often sought for, many times may be hard to discern. God will speak to us when needed, although rarely does it come in strictly verbal direction. It may be through a simple thought, a picture, or a particular

---

[19] Galatians 5:22 (NIV).

scripture that comes to mind. Listening for the voice of the Lord takes a bit of practice, maturity, and spiritual integrity. I have always been a bit dubious of anyone who says they hear the voice of the Lord all the time or have a direct "pipeline to God."

Having said all this, one thing we know is that obedience is hard, but when practiced well, it is well rewarded. When Job obediently acknowledged God's absolute omnipotence, the Lord restored Job's fortunes by a factor of two. When Naaman, commander of the Army of Aram, had leprosy, by doing just as Elisha has ordered—dipping himself in the Jordan River seven times—his skin disease was healed.[20] We may not always see our physical "recompense" as Job did, or a healing as Naaman resolutely received, but rest assured, we will be rewarded—be it in this world or the one to come. Besides, as we become more obedient, we grow closer to Him, and isn't that the greatest gift or recompense of all? Amen. So be it!

---

[20] 2 Kings 5:13–14 (NIV).

John D. Emens, PhD

DOUBLE-EDGED BLESSING

God gave us free will as well as an independent, unique spirit; this is a good thing. At the same time, self-sufficiency is good up unto a point—that point until we no longer feel we need the Lord. It is all too easy in this modern, post-materialist, industrialized world—where most of our physical needs are met—to no longer feel like we need God. Good job, nice house, shiny car, good family, and good health—where is there room to require divine succor? Even worse, we may not just ignore God; we may rebel against the Lord by finding ourselves doing things we shouldn't do or things that are offensive to our Maker.

The Israelites had all their needs met, and then they perfunctorily strayed and went their own way:

Forty years you sustained them in the wilderness so that they lacked nothing; their clothes did not wear out and their feet did not swell. And you gave them kingdoms and peoples, and allotted to them every corner, so they took possession of the land. (Nehemiah 9:21–22 NRSV)

They were disobedient and rebelled ... Therefore you gave them into the hands of their enemies, who made them suffer ... they cried out to you and you heard them from heaven, and according to your great mercies you gave them saviors who saved them from the hands of their enemies ... But after they had rest, they again did evil before you, and you abandoned them to the hands of their enemies ... yet when they turned and cried to you, you heard from heaven, and many times you rescued them according to your mercies ... And you warned them in order to turn them back to your law. Yet they acted presumptuously and did not obey your commandments, but sinned against your ordinances. (Nehemiah 9:27–29 NRSV)

Back and forth the Israelites went, from obedience to disobedience, from right relationship to wrong relationship. From good comfort to abject neediness and back again. Just like a yo-yo. Ugh!

Blessings can seem like a double-edged sword. The better we do—the more God in His favor rewards us—the more we tend to stray or drift away, and God must bring blight. When creature comforts are high, our incipient need for God feels low. It is that simple. We look only to the gifts and not the giver. Soon, we feel we don't need the "giver" at all, so we ignore God completely. Then, it seems God has a choice—to let us drift or throw us a curve or roadblock to get our attention and win us back.

As strange as it sounds, in His mercy, He may cause us difficulty or suffering. In doing so—like He did with the Israelites—through duress, He prompts and gives us the opportunity to come back to Him. If we continue to ignore Him, He allows us to go our own way due to free will. If we never come back, we shipwreck our faith. Yet, there is still hope. As it says in Hosea 14:4, "I will heal their backsliding" (NKJV). The New American Standard translation of this passage actually says, "I will heal their apostasy." Second Timothy 2:13 reads, "If we are faithless, he remains faithful for he cannot disown Himself" (NIV).

Even if we give up on God, He doesn't give up on us. However, just because God can give us a long leash—or is patient with us when we stray—it doesn't give us license for abject, chronic disobedience. Make no mistake, God is love, but He can also be fire. When we ignore or rebel without a care, it is disrespectful to Him. He made us. As hard as it is for us to swallow at times, the undeniable truth is that He calls the shots. When we disagree with this truism, we put ourselves on the throne—and we put ourselves at odds with our Maker. As Proverbs 9:10 reminds us, "The fear of the Lord is the beginning of wisdom" (NIV). So, let us be wise!

John D. Emens, PhD

INVENTORY

It is true; we all can do good things. Some of us do wonderful things, but we all also err at times. James 3:2 says, "For all us make many mistakes" (NRSV). Another translation reads: "For we all often stumble and fall and offend in many things" (Amplified). When we hurt others, we temporarily fall into wrong relationship with God. Upon occurrence, we either deal with these foibles directly or push them down and repress them; in the latter case, such deep wounds may fester and come back to haunt us in other ways.

It is best to deal with these issues directly and openly. As it says in James 5:16: "Confess to one another your faults (your slips, your false steps, your offenses, your sins) and pray [also] for one another, that you may be healed and restored [to a spiritual tone of mind and heart]. The earnest (heartfelt, continued) prayer of a righteous man makes tremendous power available [dynamic in its working]" (Amplified). There is healing power in bringing wrongs into the open and dealing with them accordingly. As it says in the beginning of the Gospel of John (1:5), "The light shines in the darkness, and the darkness has not overcome it" (NRSV).

So, we need to take an inventory of our lives, rectify missteps, and acknowledge wrongdoing. At the same time, where others have hurt, maligned, or disparaged us, we need to deal with this too. Whether we confront a perpetrator of the wrong or not, we need to forgive, which may not be easy to do, and in doing so, we can find peace.

When we don't forgive others—even if they don't ask for forgiveness—we are the true emotional victim. Only by pardoning them and letting go do we become truly free. If we have wronged others, we must have the wherewithal to ask forgiveness from them; in doing so, we free ourselves from nagging guilt and self-recriminations.

Like confessing to the Lord, confessing to others brings relief. Confessed sin brings forgiveness and redemption. As it says in Psalm 32:5: "I will confess my transgressions to the Lord [continually unfolding the past till all is told]—then You [instantly] forgave the guilt and iniquity of my sin" (Amplified). The result of confession and absolution is personal peace and tranquility. We all make mistakes, but if we humble ourselves and fess up our mistakes, we get a clean slate. Life truly can be a "do-over." And unquestionably, do-overs are a good thing.

Galatians 5:1 says, "It is for freedom that Christ has set you free" (NIV). So, do a personal inventory, check your emotional dresser drawer, and look for any dirty smelly socks; we all have them. Let's clean house!

OVERDUE HOLIDAY

The flakes of snow softly and silently parachuted to the ground. The cold, sleepy wind pushed hard against my frosty red cheeks. My warm breath billowed out heavily as I crunched step-by-step to Dad and Mom's place deep in the woods. *Janie will be there. I have not seen her since my last assignment in Kabul.* I sniff back my runny nose. *I so badly hope she likes my gift.*

I crossed the meandering path around the icy pond and went left at the big walnut tree. *I hope Janie made it to the house okay. I know she had a long drive, and I hope there was not too much traffic for her.* I paused and gazed across the broad ashen meadow only to see the large rustic cabin Dad and I built so many years ago; the well-lit windows were bright with cheer, and I could almost taste the steaming mug of hot fruited wine awaiting.

I hastened past the frozen brook where I had dunked my sister Hannah time and time again. I kept trudging along at a steady clip. I glanced up to see the tall blue spruces standing like sentries lining the walk; they were silently urging me to keep pressing on. I tried to think of the last time I was here. *It must have been two summers ago—the year of the big storm. June it was—right before I met Janie.*

I paused for a steadier heartbeat, and then I reached for the outer door. I took a deep breath and exhaled. I then beat a hearty knock on the main door. I could hear rustling, excited voices and warm music inside. In a flash, my mind remembered my upcoming assignment in Greece, and just as quickly, I pushed the thought out of my mind.

The door opened. Dad pulled me inside and gave me one of his signature bear hugs. Mom gave me a warm smile, a quick hug, and a kiss on the cheek. Hannah and her husband, Thomas, greeted me with grins. My younger sister, Sarah, hugged me, and her four kids clung to my legs for dear life. Cousin Emma and her fiancé came up to me; hugs, kisses, and proper introductions were made.

I glanced over at the fireplace, and there was Janie wearing a thick gray wool pullover and faded boot-cut Lee jeans. At first, her face was expressionless, and I swallowed convulsively. It had been a long time since I had seen her. She then gave me a pained, contorted "miss-you-so-much" broken smile, and my heart skipped a beat. Janie calmly walked up to me and placed her hands around my waist. She gave me a tender kiss on the cheek and held me tightly, just letting the tears come—from both of us. Everyone was silent, letting us have the moment. Our mouths met. Our bodies clutched together as one ... and then Janie unceremoniously passed an ice cube to me, mouth to mouth.

"Thanks," I mumbled.

"That's what you get for being late!" Janie slyly replied, her mouth breaking into a broad, engaging smile. She winked.

I scratched my head and laughed out loud. *Business as usual.* I managed a broad, impish grin as I followed Janie to the hearth to join the whole family for our annual Christmas toast.

CLOSE SHAVE

Two days ago, during dialysis, my fistula failed. A fistula is a catheter or "port" in my arm where an artery has been surgically connected to a vein to provide a vessel to draw a continuous flow of blood for the dialysis process.

When I then went into surgery the following day for a "fistula gram" to "tune up" the compromised vessel, the surgeon soon discovered the fistula was "clogged" and completely unusable. What was supposed to be a simple ten-minute procedure, turned into a two-hour medical rescue mission. The likely or probable outcome of the situation was a completely failed catheter in my arm, and the necessity of putting a temporary catheter or port in my chest, which was not the least bit desirable.[21] By the grace of God, the skilled surgeon was able to unclog the vessel by using multiple angioplasties, thereby widening the artery to improve blood flow. The surgery was a success, and by the grace of God, I knew I had dodged a major medical bullet. Therefore, this morning, I was able to resume my midweek dialysis treatment.

Yes, it was a bit of a close shave for me yesterday, but the Lord saw me through it. Like Daniel in the Bible, the Lord delivered me from the medical mouths of the lions of what could have been much more compromised health condition. As I pondered my gratitude for the outcome of the procedure, Psalm 34:19 came to mind: "Many are the afflictions of the righteous, but the Lord delivers him out of them all" (ESV). But that thought would imply that I am righteous, and I am, but not on my own account. It is but only by the blood of the Lamb, Lord Jesus Christ.

Yet one wonders, why did God so adroitly "heal" my fistula situation

---

[21] It is much preferable to have a catheter in one's arm than in one's chest for reasons of physical freedom and the much reduced chance of dangerous internal infection.

but fail to combat my ankle infection, which caused me to lose my leg? Why did He allow the antibiotics used to try to save the leg end up killing my kidneys and putting me in dialysis at the age of fifty-seven? The answer to that question is simple yet confounding. We don't know—God is God. The currents and eddies of life—the ups and downs and the triumphs and tragedies—are a giant mystery. The Lord is the only one who knows and understands the solution to this grand puzzle.

My little fistula situation in the grand scheme of the paradigm of the whole universe is infinitesimally small, yet I know because it is important to me, it is important to Him. I know I am in the palm of His hand. Even though He can close His hand and crush me at any time, He doesn't. He treasures me and everyone else on this planet. God is a Creator, Protector, Deliverer, but He is also an Orchestra Director. He calls the shots, and we dance to His tune. Sometimes He gives, and sometimes He takes away. I must only obediently trust in Him and call Him Lord; that is all He asks in order to make a room reservation for me at the last stop on this bemusing, uncertain, precarious river of life. Fortunately, on this river, He is the water as well as the boat. He also provides us with a paddle for prayers to help us successfully navigate each day's dangerous rapids.

The good news is that even if we fall out of the boat, He is not just our God—He is our life preserver!

John D. Emens, PhD

STOP BELIEVING IN GOD!

Stop believing in God! Why do I say this? It's simple. I don't believe in God. I don't believe in Jesus Christ at all. Rather, I *know* Him. Huh. Does that sound bold? Does it sound audacious to really know God? How do I know the Lord? I know God the same way one knows how to do almost anything in life. I follow directions. For example, when making food, I simply follow a recipe. For example, when making McCormick sausage-flavor country gravy, I pour the contents of the packet in a large bowl, slowly stir in two cups of cold water, and stir vigorously with a whisk. After I add the cooked sausage, I slowly bring it to a boil until it thickens with an occasional stir. Once thickened, voila! We have sausage gravy. I believe I have the gravy, but how do I know it? I taste it, and if it tastes right, then I know I have sausage gravy. And when I eat the gravy, and it tastes good, I know that I know that I know everything about that gravy mix is true.

When knowing God, it starts in many ways with the right recipe: the scriptures. Coming to know God is in many ways just following directions. First by reading what we know what we have to do. We want to understand just what Jesus did for us. By reading, we see there was a flaw in the design of humans—sin—and it can be overcome by understanding the joining of the imperfect (us) with the perfect (Him).

The design flaw causes death, but this can be overcome by adding the right ingredient to the mix: adding the blood of the cross to neutralize and cover any of our sins. This blood can be added into the mix by anyone by the verbal asking, and the result of this asking is salvation—eternal life. The recipe in Romans 10:9 specifically reads: "If you confess with your mouth that Jesus is Lord and believe in your heart that God raised him from the dead, you will be saved" (ESV).

When we do this asking, the Holy Spirit comes into our hearts to give us a true physical joining with our eternal Maker. Like physical spaceships docking in orbit, our spirits will join. And like water added to the McCormick mix, we will have not gravy, but something better: peace. We will be able to actually taste the peace that "passeth all understanding." Voila! The proof is in the pudding.

A second way to know God is to follow the recipe on the box, the Bible, and actually watch how others do it. The thief on the cross who was dying next to Jesus saw the Lord forgiving our sins as we stoned him to death. Luke 23:24 notes that while dying, Christ said, "Father, forgive them for they know not what they do" (KJV). Watching the situation, it reports in Luke 23:42, the thief simply said to Jesus, "Remember me when you come into your kingdom" (NIV). Note the word *kingdom*, which means the thief recognized Jesus as "King" or Lord. Having heard this request, Jesus looked at the thief, and in Luke 23:43, he replied, "Today you will be with me in paradise" (NIV). This statement meant the thief would be in heaven forever. We too can have salvation; it is there for the asking. Simply say, "Lord Jesus, please come into my heart as my personal Savior. I repent or turn away from my sins and wrongdoings. Please be the Lord of my life. Amen." By saying this, the Holy Spirit physically comes into our beings, we can taste the peace of the Lord, and most importantly, we have salvation—eternal life!

Finally, the third way of knowing God is simply by worldly experiences. Once we ask the Lord into our lives, we can see Him working in so many ways over and over again. For me, it may be something small in the "normal" or something big in the supernatural. For example, something mundane might be an unexpected blessing like not getting that speeding ticket or actually getting a cash refund on an expensive defective retail item at Wal-Mart without a receipt, which is next to impossible. Seeing God at work with something big might be like when my close relative had her large abdominal tumor inexplicably "disappear" after the x-ray had previously designated its clear existence in her midsection.

So, stop believing in God—and start knowing Him. Remember that He is a person (or persons, actually) with feelings. He can be pleased, and He can have His feelings hurt. He flashes anger at injurious wrongdoings, like when He observes child abuse, and He bubbles joy when a new believer comes into new relationship with Him. He loves adoration and hates to be ignored. He will not be mocked, and He is inexplicably patient with all our foibles.

Most of all, no matter what we do, He is a proud Daddy. Like all fathers, He will be overjoyed to see us when we come though heaven's gates, and He will lavish love and splendor onto us upon our arrival. As the apostle Paul writes in 1 Corinthians 2:9: "No eye has seen no ear has heard, and no mind has imagined the things God has prepared for those who love Him" (ISV).

MISUNDERSTOOD
DANDELION

It is just past the ides of March in Ohio, a bright, sun-splashed Sunday morn. Birds are tweeting. Fresh buds are just sprouting on tree limbs. Check the phone: thirty-nine degrees outside—still a brisk chill in the air. Can see the grass getting greener. Yep, it is about time for the dandelions to pop up—the misunderstood dandelions.

Some folks think dandelions are flowers, but they are actually weeds. Dandelions will soon spread over our lawn like a buttery sheen, glistening and dripping off of a steaming hot ear of yellow corn. We get at least a thousand of these pesky unwelcome lawn guests from May to August. We say "unwelcome," but methinks these gentle dandelions are most beautiful.

These bright maize blooms squat proud, upright as bright buttercup buttons flanked by moist, green-tongued fronds, which spill out around them in bouquet fashion, kissing up toward the bright azure sky. Surrounded by crisp, moist white clover, which almost looks like baby's breath from a floral arrangement, the dandelions stand tall, almost mocking the frustrated homeowner who tries to eradicate them completely. With roots down deep, the dandelion knows it is just like a resilient starfish in the ocean; cutting off one piece is just a pruning, and it only causes more of them to grow back quickly.

Yet dandelions are indeed misunderstood because although they are a pesky pest and irritant to many, they are actually pacifist in nature; they only want to coexist with the lush, supple verdant sod as a compatriot, not a neighborhood complaint. "Live and let live," the dandelion spews to the rooftops, only wanting a stay of execution before the TruGreen or Barefoot Grass dudes appear. "Please," they beg, "Yank my top only." That way, they

John D. Emens, PhD

can live for another day. Stems on their knees, they implore the aggressor, the homeowner, for mercy just to live and breathe for one moment longer. Once proud and sassy, the victim dandelion now becomes sepulcher silent as the chemical spraying begins. Praying for an ensuing deluge of rain to dilute the chemical warfare, the dandelion only hopes there will be a few sole survivors to tell the tale after the homeowner's holocaust has begun.

All the misunderstood dandelion wanted was to live, to grow, and to befriend the unkind world—and overcome evil with goodness. Unable to mollify its enemies, it accepts is fate graciously, and it places its harmless, humble yellow head in the noose of modern horticultural science. It regrets dying, but it knows in its heart that come next spring, it will have one more chance to shine. The dandelion sports a wan smile as its head begins to bow, and then its withering rumpled leaves turn spotty brown.

Rest in peace, little dandelions. Rest in peace. You are not alone—none of us like being judged or misunderstood!

HOT COALS

In Proverbs 25:21–22, it reads, "If your enemy is hungry, give him bread to eat; and if he is thirsty, give him water to drink. For in doing so, you will heap coals of fire upon his head, and the Lord will reward you" (Amplified). Apostle Paul cites this passage of scripture, and in Romans 12:21, he adds, "Do not let yourself be overcome with evil, but overcome (master) evil with good [Amplified]. Huh? Pray for your enemies? It seems more appropriate to do the opposite!

Truth be known, it isn't always easy to pray for our enemies, and it seems more natural to pray *against* our enemies. But when you pray for blessings upon your enemies, God may bless them by giving them "true" hot coals in the form of affliction, difficulty, and strife. Not always, but if your enemies are unbelievers, God can be "cruel to be kind." He may knock them down a couple of notches to put them in a position where they may someday believe.

Humility is the necessary precursor to one's asking the Lord into their life to be their personal Savior. Prideful people don't worship anybody or anything—except perhaps themselves—and a few hot coals might be just what the doctor ordered to get them so they might look to the heavens for assistance. Think of it as godly tough love.

We want others to come to know the joy, peace, and love of salvation. We may need to show them acceptance and love, even if it is hard to do, and we can do this by praying blessings upon them. It is totally up to God to decide in what form those blessings might be. Committing your enemies into God's hands may be your part in His whole plan to rescue others and make you more whole in the process.

John D. Emens, PhD

If we feel persecuted by others, we may, in the end, just have to let go and pray His will be done. He did say in John 16:33, "In this world you will have trouble" (NIV). If trouble is a person or persons, then He is clear: pray blessing upon them. Then let Him take over.

Christ did command us to love the unlovable—and that starts with loving our enemies.

QUARTERBACK
CONTROVERSY

(Fictitious story with fictitious characters)

Rex Danielson placed his hands under center and barked out the signals, "T-41, T-41, hut, hut, hut!" The center snapped the football, and Danielson faded back, taking a five-step drop, and then looked downfield. He wanted to go to Nate Neuroth on the out pattern, but it was covered. So, with defensive linemen in his face, he checked it down to the running back Williamson in the flat. "Willie" (as he was called) was promptly tackled by the Steelers' linebacker and laid flat on his back. The play was a loss of four yards. It was now second down and fourteen yards to go. "Not good," Rex murmured. It was the last game of the preseason, and this was his last chance to make the team. Rex knew he was in a battle for the third quarterback position on the depth chart to make it with Green Bay Packers. He knew if he got cut from the Packers, he would probably end up on some practice squad in God-knows-where. As he was listening in his helmet for the next play, he prayed to the Lord, "God, just help me get this ball in the end zone so I can make the team. Please!"

Danielson got the next play, went into the shotgun, and barked the signals, "T-17, T-17." Immediately Rex noticed the Steelers' safety on the left flank come creeping toward the line of scrimmage; it looked like a safety blitz. He knew he could get Garbo on a skinny post. He changed the play. He barked, "Houston 67, Houston 67." He lifted his heel, and wide receiver Garbo ran behind him and went into the slot position on the strong side. "Hut-hut-hut!" The center snapped the ball. Rex faded back, and in doing so, he saw the safety blitzing on the weak side. Danielson

John D. Emens, PhD

rolled out right out of the pocket to buy some time. He saw Garbo breaking past his defender, and Rex drilled the ball to the center of the field and held his breath. Garbo went up for the ball … completion! First down! Twenty-three-yard gain.

It was now first and ten on the Steelers' forty-seven yard line. Rex got the next play, which was a halfback counter that gained a good nine yards. It was second and one for a first down. The call from the sidelines was for a fullback dive, but Rex thought, *Hey, this is a waste down. I can go for something if I see something weak in the Steelers' secondary because we've still got third down to get the first.*

Rex went under center. He surveyed the field. The linebackers were crowded in to stop the run, and the safeties were in a soft cover-two.

This is my moment! Rex thought. At the line of scrimmage, Rex changed the play; he yelled the audible, "Texas 22! Blackjack 42, Blackjack 42, hut, hut, hut!" Rex took the snap from center, faked to the fullback using play action, and faded back in a deep drop. He looked to his left to decoy the strong safety and then threw a long ball to the right where Neuroth was streaking down the sidelines on a fly pattern. Neuroth broke free, and the pass was perfect; it landed softly into the receiver's hands. Neuroth snatched the ball out of the air and danced untouched into the end zone. Touchdown!

The stadium went wild. The fans were cheering, and the bench mobbed Rex and Nate Neuroth when they got to the bench. Rex and Nate— also a rookie trying out for the team—hugged each other and high-fived themselves half a dozen times. It was a total celebration on the Green Bay Packer sideline!

As it turned out, Rex's touchdown pass to Nate was the game-winning score. In the locker room after the game, Rex saw that Nate Neuroth still had the football that he had caught in the end zone. It was Nate's first professional touchdown catch, and he understandably wanted to keep the ball. Rex stood from the far end of the locker room as Nate put the ball into his locker and left the changing area. Rex felt a deep pang of envy; his pass to Nate Neuroth was the only professional touchdown pass he had ever thrown. He definitely wanted to keep the ball for himself.

Rex took an extra-long shower. It just burned him up that Nate got the football instead of him. *At least Neuroth could have discussed it with me first. For goodness' sake, I threw it to him!*

As he dressed, Rex wondered about his chances of making the team. After his touchdown pass, he knew he probably had things sewn up. *Yep, I'm probably a shoo-in.*

Rex started walking out the locker room door, and then he hesitated. He realized he was the last one in the locker area. He paused, stopped, and bit his lip. *Man, I want to be able to show my friends and family the actual football that was my first professional touchdown!*

He furtively looked about, turned, and quietly went back into the locker room. Rex unceremoniously walked over to Nate's unlocked locker and purloined the football. He carefully put the ball in his gym bag, and he sauntered off the Packer premises. With feigned nonchalance, he got into his car and drove to his apartment.

Once inside his place, he pulled out the football, kissed it, and sat down in a huff on the sofa. He touched the football over and over again until he eventually fell asleep on the sofa. Before he winked out, he quietly and thankfully said the Lord's Prayer and thanked God for the touchdown pass completion and for the football now safely in his possession. Soon Rex Danielson gratefully fell into in a deep slumber.

The next morning, the ringing of Rex's cell phone awoke him out of his deep sleep. As he picked up his phone, he realized he had overslept. Wiping his sandy eyes, Rex said, "Hello?"

The voice on the phone was the Packer GM, Bob Westmore. "Good morning, Rex."

In that moment, Rex figured he had made the team. "Yes. Hello, Mr. Westmore. How are you?"

"Fine Rex. Just fine. But I don't quite know how to say this, but the Packers are going to go with Carson."

Rex replied, "What are you saying? That you picked Carson Gibbons as the third backup quarterback instead of me? Does that mean you are letting me go? Cutting me?"

There was a long pause, and then Westmore replied, "Yes, Rex, we are letting you go. I am very sorry. You are a good kid, and you've got a pretty good arm. Tremendous touchdown pass you threw last night. I am sure someone else will pick you up. Goodbye and good luck. Click!"

John D. Emens, PhD

Rex clicked his phone off and put his head his hands. He was stunned. What would he do? Where would he go? He got up off the sofa, and he knew he had to call his family and tell them the bad news. He felt embarrassed and ashamed. In college, he came from a Power5 conference and was a fifth-round pick. He couldn't believe he didn't make the team. He paced around the apartment, finally sitting down on the sofa in quiet exasperation. He was ready to cry. He looked over to the coffee table, and he spied the football. Ever so slowly, he started to feel guilty about stealing the ball from Nate. Sure, he rationalized that it was *his* throw, so it should be *his* ball. Yet, as a believer in the Lord, he knew he shouldn't have taken if from Nate without his permission. Guilt began to nag at him deep into his bosom.

After thinking it over long and hard, Rex decided to find a way to give the ball back to Nate. Rex knew he would have to explain how he had taken it in the first place, and a heartfelt apology would have to be forthcoming. Rex called Nate's apartment.

The receiver's roommate, Blaine Wilkerson, answered the phone.

Rex asked if Nate was available, and Blaine replied, "He is at practice."

Rex said "Thanks. Goodbye."

Huh? Nate is at practice. That means he made the team.

Rex walked over to the front window of his apartment and looked out. It was raining. A soft, sad August rain. He thought for a moment, and then knew what he had to do. He went over to his desk and wrote out an apology note. He put the football and the note in his gym bag and drove to the Packer football complex. The locker room was empty since the team was still out on the field. Rex placed the football and the apology note in Nate's locker and then hightailed it out of there.

Driving back to his apartment, Rex, although feeling sheepish and embarrassed, actually felt better—he had done right thing. His guilt lifted, his mind turned toward the future. What would he do? Tuck his tail between his legs and go home? He wondered if he should call up Westmore and beg the Packers to put him on their practice squad. Maybe he could get a local job in town doing whatever and try out again next year. "Lord, help me!" he silently prayed.

A moment later, Rex's cell phone rang. Rex normally wouldn't answer a call while driving, but something told him to reconsider. It was an out-of-state area code—probably a robocall—but Rex picked it up anyway. "Hello, this is Rex."

A voice said, "Rex Danielson, this is Vince Payback with the Cleveland Browns."

"Yes, Mr. Payback, what can I do for you?"

"Well, we just lost our third-string quarterback to a torn ACL in the last preseason game yesterday. The Cleveland Browns would like to extend an offer to you to join our team."

Long pause.

"Rex, are you there?"

"Um. Yes. Yes, I would like to play for the Cleveland Browns. I accept your offer."

"Great, Rex. I will have my assistant, Tara, talk to your agent to discuss contract terms. Is that acceptable to you?"

"Absolutely! Yes. Thank you, Mr. Payback."

"You are very welcome Rex, and by the way, welcome to the Cleveland Browns."

Click.

Rex swerved into a nearby McDonald's and parked. Before he bowed his head to pray a thank you to the Lord for the blessing that had just fallen into his lap, he glanced at the passenger seat. Sitting on the empty seat was the open gym bag, which had previously held the returned football. In that instant, it hit him. Rex realized the hard truth that one reaps what one sows, and he had done the right thing in giving the football back to Nate Neuroth. In doing so, the Lord reciprocated. Yes, there are consequences to our actions. Rex turned his eyes heavenward and smiled. His dream had finally come true: he was going to play professional football in the National Football League. More importantly though, Rex knew he was in God's good graces again—and that was the best feeling of all.

ASHES

Sometimes it is easy to question whether we are good enough for God to use us in a meaningful or productive way, especially when going through a rough or dry season. At moments like this, it is helpful to look at how the Lord used so many imperfect and flawed people in the Bible to do amazing things.

If you look at the "greats" in the scriptures, you might be surprised. Moses murdered an Egyptian. David killed one of his own officers in order to take the man's wife. Paul imprisoned and perpetrated murder for many, many Christians. Noah was a drunk, and Matthew was a tax collector who beat up poor people for money. Mary Magdalene was a prostitute, as was Rahab, the Canaanite, who saved Israelite spies from the enemy, the king of Jericho. Jonah was a resolute coward, and Israelite King Saul threw spears at young David trying to kill him out of sheer jealousy. Finally, Judas was a thief, allegedly stealing money from the disciples' money bag, as well was a traitor for handing Jesus over to be tried and crucified. Judas, like all these aforementioned folks, was a pivotal player in God's ultimate plan. The same is true for us; like all these biblical persons, we have a special, specific role to play for Lord. A unique destiny.

Yes, over and over, God uses weak or flawed persons in the scriptures to fulfill His objectives. He ends up redeeming most of these people in one form or another. This should give us hope. The Lord can use us wherever we are in our walks—even if we are not at our best or if we are struggling.

Even in our worst circumstances, we can still be a blessing to others. As a new amputee, I was a bit dejected about having to start dialysis. My wise wife said, "Jack, maybe God wants you to be in that dialysis room to minister to people there—maybe that's your new calling. Stop being a crybaby!" It is easy to wonder why God allows us to muddle and struggle.

Yet, many times, only by looking back in retrospect can we see the beauty and logic to His plans. Take heart, for wherever you are, no matter how you feel, God can use you mightily!

After a raging forest fire, all that is left are the ashes. Ash will create the most fertile soil for growth of future flora and fauna, and the same applies to us! Never count yourself out. Wherever you are, be a blessing to others!

CHRIST'S HOUR

In *A Lifting Up for the Downcast* (1648), William Bridges is a Catholic priest who, during the bubonic plague, does his level best to encourage others by writing edifying essays of hope. He argues that no matter what the circumstance, one should never be dejected or "downcast." Over and over, he delineates how we should find positive ways of looking at things even when hope seems completely lost. Near the close of his book, Bridges asserts that in the end—even if we are at the end of our rope, even if it seems that all else is failing, and even if we have totally exhausted all avenues for any positive outcome and there is no hope at all—then it is "Christ's hour." God will be our rescuer. The Lord will be our champion. We can count on Him.

I think we all can look back in our lives to recall a few "Christ hours." I can. And when our lives wind down, and we come close to the end, we can have hope that He will be there waiting for us on the other side. Final redemption will be an incredible, very beautiful thing indeed.

At the end of his life, Paul found himself in a bit of a quandary. To paraphrase, he said he wished to be with the Lord, but in Philippians 1:23–24, he stated, "But to remain in the flesh is more necessary for you [one of his young Christian churches]" (NRSV). I can relate to this outlook since my life is winding down as well. I will keep doing the one thing I can do, which is put pen to paper. I will continue writing as long as He wills me to.

So, no matter where you are in your life—no matter what age or season of life—remember you are not alone. In good times and bad, He walks every step with you. He will stand by you. As Jesus said when He departed from His disciples in Matthew 20:20: "I am with you always, to the end of the Age" (NRSV). And until the very end of time, if by chance you are in a quandary or a bad fix, remember that when all else seems lost—it is "Christ's hour" indeed!

PIT, PITIFUL,
SELF-PITY, PUL-PIT

"Pit" means "Hades" or "Sheol" or "a low or wretched psychological state," as defined by the Oxford Dictionary. Whether "pit" is a place we don't want to be or an extraordinarily difficult physical, mental, or emotional compromised state, it is a situation we want to avoid. The psalmist writes in Psalm 40:2: "He drew me out of a horrible pit [a pit of tumult and destruction], out of the miry clay (froth and slime), and set my feet upon a rock, steadying my steps and establishing my goings" (Amplified).

The problem is that when we are in the pit, usually due to onerous circumstances such as sickness, job loss, divorce, relationship trauma, or pecuniary difficulties, we all run the risk of self-pity. Self-pity, rightly understood, is just a person feeling sorry for themselves. We can all understand or empathize with someone when they take a hit and are down for a while, but self-pity—even when you are in a pit—is the enemy. It is easy to do, but it is actually a prideful, self-serving state of mind and being. In self-pity, one is actually saying, "Why has this happened to me? I don't deserve to be in this situation." The more time one spends looking inward, the less time one is spending solving and finding a way out a problematic situation. Self-pity, uncorrected or not, leads to self-defeat.

Self-dejection and inward sorrow toward oneself is called "navel gazing," and it is just plain pitiful. "Pitiful" is an adjective defined as being "very small, or poor, or inadequate," with synonyms being "paltry, miserable, meager, beggarly, and insufficient" (Oxford Dictionary). In the scriptures, we can think of many folks in pitiful situations, including Joseph being imprisoned for a crime he did not commit or Job losing everything.

John D. Emens, PhD

Job's health was so bad that he had sores all over his body. In Job 30:30 he writes, "My skin falls from me in blackened flakes, and my bones are burned with heat." Job writes in 33:21 "[My] flesh is so wasted away that … [my] bones that were not seen stick out" (both Amplified).

Poor Jonah ended up in the belly of a whale, and Stephen was unceremoniously stoned to death. Yet, we can take heart for in each of these "pitiful" cases the protagonist was, to some extent, redeemed.

Joseph ended up as prime minister of Egypt, Job's fortunes were doubled, and Jonah finally exonerated himself by delivering God's message to Nineveh. Stephen was dubbed a saint vis-à-vis his martyr's death, and he ascended into heaven. God provides redemption for followers in pitiable situations, and He leaves no one in the lurch. This should give us pause, and upon reflection, we can no doubt see pitiful situations in our own lives where, in retrospect, the Lord has delivered us or redeemed in big or small ways.

When we come through the fire, and our conflicts are resolved, our "test" becomes our "testimony." Our "pit" becomes ripe fodder to brag about God's deliverance as we speak from our "pul-pit." From the pulpit, we can call others on and ease the furrowed brows of those who currently are in a pit or pitiable circumstances. Yes, there is purpose to our pain no matter how pitiful our circumstances may seem at the time.

By avoiding the culprit—self-pity—we get out of the pitiable pit, and with redemption, we tell our triumphs from our pulpits. Sounds "pritty" good to me.

TOOTHPASTE TRUTH

A typical store-bought tube of toothpaste seems to last forever—kinda like our human lives. By careful judicious use of the toothpaste—like taking good care of our minds and bodies—we think we can avoid eventual discontinuation, i.e., death. Au contraire. Even though we squeeze and press to the utmost, at some point, the tube doth run out and expire—just like our lives. Bang! Life over. We can always purchase another tube of toothpaste. Regrettably, we cannot buy another life. Nope, even with a sale price, there is only one available per customer.

Think about the veracity of this toothpaste metaphor the next time you brush your teeth!

John D. Emens, PhD

Us

As Christians, we know there is a bifurcation in the Bible, namely, the Old Testament and the New Testament. We think of the Old Testament as the introduction of God the Father and His ongoing relationship to us humans through His commitment to the nation of Israel. We see the New Testament as the coming of the Messiah, Jesus Christ, as a fulfillment of the covenant He promised from Abraham to Isaiah and to the other prophets. The Old Testament is about Yahweh, the God I Am. The New Testament is an expression of God the Father's love for us through His Son, Jesus Christ, and expressed directly into our hearts as believers through the Holy Spirit.

Yet, Jesus Christ is also in the Old Testament. Genesis 1:26 says, "Then God said, 'Let Us make man in Our image, according Our likeness'" (NKJV). The key word here is "us." Plural. Yes, God is more than one. The Amplified translation of this verse is this: "God said, 'Let Us [Father, Son, and Holy Spirit] make mankind in Our image, and after Our likeness.'"

The scriptures could not be clearer: Jesus Christ is in the Old Testament. This truth is also mirrored in the beginning of the Gospel of John (1:1): "In the beginning [before all time] was the Word (Christ), and the Word was with God, and the Word was God Himself" (Amplified). Yes, Jesus Christ was there in the very beginning with Father God. And, yes, Jesus will be with Father God in the end—as will we!

Some people say the Trinity is not specifically in the Bible. I say look again!

CAN'T WIN FOR LOSING

It's now the year 2040, and there are no more competitions of any kind. The government decided a decade earlier to abolish winners and losers. So, they took any competition out of schools and classrooms. Public schools and colleges eliminated grades and class rankings. No more National Honor Society or valedictorians. No more honor roll or dean's lists in college. Private schools soon followed suit. Team sports were allowed to continue, but games had no scoring. All swimming and track events were not timed. Everyone was given a participation trophy just for being on a team. In professional sports, the new approach also was mandated. All football, basketball, baseball, and soccer games could be held, but the scores were no longer counted. Everybody just played for fun. Everybody was a winner.

Soon, this new approach spilled over to the rest of the world. All jobs paid the same hourly wages. Everybody had the same job title even if job descriptions were different. Doctors, movie stars, and professional athletes all made the same amount of money as garbage collectors and fast-food employees. The president of the United States made precisely the same amount as a city cop. There was no minimum wage—only a standard wage for all. No promotions and no one could lose their job for any reason.

It worked for a while until students stopped studying. Athletes stopped trying. Professional sports no longer drew attendance in stadiums and coliseums. No one cared to watch games when players weren't competing. Businesses fell apart because employees were paid whether they showed up or not. Industrial production came to a standstill. Farming and agribusinesses halted, and people returned to hunting and gathering. There was a mass migration out of cities and into the countryside as folks foraged for food and scarce resources. Government fell apart as workers left their city jobs in search of hinterland necessities. Anarchy prevailed.

Yes, it is now 2040. People are wearing animal furs and organizing into local tribes. Looks like humankind has come full circle. Yep, nobody is a loser now. We are all the same now—all of us are unhappy, unfed, and unhealthy. Paradise lost indeed.

DO NOT FORGET THE LORD

Imagine your typical reasonably affluent parent who is nearing the end of their life. They set out to make out their will and designate their inheritance. They plan wisely and with great forethought. They know that what they leave to their children will provide them with many blessings for years to come—at least that is their hope. Then suppose the parent's health declines, and he or she is put into a nursing facility. Suppose none of the children ever visit over long periods of time—maybe just once per year at best. How will that parent feel? He or she had thought out and planned to give a great deal of money to their children, yet their kids won't even come to visit? Looks like the inheritance might be better used somewhere else—maybe to the parent's church or favorite charity where it might be more appreciated and more gratefully received.

This little made-up story is analogous to God and the way He looks at us when considering giving us gifts. He wants us to look to Him—the Giver—and not just the gifts. If all we want is what He provides and we do not worship Him, He feels, well, slighted and ignored. God's love is unconditional, but His blessings aren't. Full stop.

Having said this, let us look to Jerimiah 29:11–13. Many of us are familiar with these verses:

For surely I know the plans I have for you, says the Lord, plans for your welfare and not for harm, to give you a future with hope. Then when you call upon me and come pray to me, I will hear you. When you search for me, you will find me; if you seek me with all your heart, I will let you find me, says the Lord, and will restore your fortunes. (NRSV)

John D. Emens, PhD

There are many important things to note in this scriptural passage, namely the words "if," "then," and "when." First, God has good thoughts and plans for us. "Then," when we pray, He will listen. "When" we seek Him with all our hearts, He will restore our fortunes. Getting the "fortunes" is predicated on an "if." Namely, "if" we seek Him with all our hearts, then He will bless us. Clearly it is a conditional blessing, but it is also understandable. If we seek and love Him first, He will bless us accordingly.

The second thing to note is that God says "me" six times in this passage. Remember, God made us—created us—for Him. So, understandably, He wants some attention from us. It's like getting a dog from a pet store. We get the canine because we want companionship around the house, apartment, or farm. We don't get a dog that will completely ignore us or run away after it gets its first bowl of food. Likewise, God expects a certain amount of praise, worship, fellowship, friendship, and adoration from us—and He deserves it! If we do love Him, He is more willing to bless us more than our fair share. If we ignore Him, we risk losing some of His favor. It is that simple. Truly.

He has given us salvation for the asking. Isn't this worth giving Him a fair bit of due glory and praise? Typically, we have a great divide where God is saying not to forget Him, and we Christians are saying, "Us, us, us!" There is the rub. We need to hit our knees and praise and bless Him—not for what He can give us but for what He has already done for us through sending His Son. God is beautiful in and of Himself; for this reason alone, He is so worthy of worship for truly the Lord is good. So, do not forget Him.

So, love God for God. Seek Him will all your heart. Bless Him, and He will bless you!

THE TWENTY-FOOT HOP

A friend of mine once told me about results he read in the paper regarding events from a recent Special Olympics. He remarked there had been an event called "the fifty-inch crawl." At the time, the notion of such an athletic event seemed ludicrous, but when one realizes that someone might be severely physically or mentally challenged (perhaps even a quadriplegic), it becomes more understandable. This is all the more realizable for me now that I am an amputee. I lost my right leg below the knee nearly three years ago. For me, I would not be in the Special Olympics; rather, I might participate in the Paralympics. My event wouldn't be the fifty-inch crawl, but perhaps it would be the "twenty-foot hop." How fast can I hop twenty feet on one leg? You see, it is all relative. What might be a challenge for one person is not for another. And we have differing expectations for each person based on their individual circumstances, talents, backgrounds, and abilities. We cannot expect a twelve-year-old child to adequately physically compete with a twenty-five-year-old professional football player, although perhaps the child could beat them at a game of chess. Every situation is different, and everyone involved should be treated and judged differently.

The same is true for us and God. He judges us individually. He has different expectations for each one of us. He doesn't expect a fourteen-year-old to be as holy or obedient as a fifty-year-old seasoned pastor, although they could be. On the other hand, the Lord might be pleased with the obedience of the experienced pastor but want him or her to have more of the "faith of child." You see, God looks at thing phenomenologically, which means He looks at each individual and their situation uniquely based on their own individual circumstances. He doesn't look just at actions; He looks at the mind, the heart, and the motive. Hence, He expects different things from different people because we each are unique and special—just

John D. Emens, PhD

like our circumstances. For my wife, a challenge might be her job or crocheting the perfect blanket. For me, it might be the twenty-foot hop, particularly if my prosthesis malfunctions unexpectedly.

The takeaway here is that we should never judge others in their walks with God. Yes, we can recognize wrongdoing, but we must not be the one pointing fingers or casting aspersions. We don't know what each person is dealing with and what issues or challenges God is putting on their plates. We shouldn't confuse our expectations for others with God's expectations for others. God deals with us in our good ways and in our bad ways on His timetable.

Ten years after I became a Christian, I married a smoker. A year later, I took up smoking, which I continued to do for a number of years. At one point, I strongly felt the Lord asking me to quit, and I did, but it was in His time and in His way. Maybe I should have quit sooner, but there were other issues in my life the Lord had me deal with first. Some people who didn't know my individual circumstances judged me harshly. This is the classic "big faith" versus "little faith." Big faith people will let God deal with people in His own way and in His own time. Little faith people will judge others based upon their own expectations and what they think should or should not be. Yes, there may be a time and place to "call" people on their sin, but by and large, it is God and the Holy Spirit who should be doing this. God sees the whole picture, from top to bottom. We don't.

As it says in Luke 6:37 (NKJV): "Judge not, and you will not be judged." Whether it is about rights, wrongs, crawls, or hops, try love!

DEATH

As a child, I remember lying in bed at night and looking up at the ceiling in the darkness and being white-hot scared to my core. My best childhood friend had just died of leukemia at the age of ten. I saw images of him in his casket and his perfectly combed brown wig carefully placed above his serene, expressionless face. Wearing his trim little boy suit with his hands folded neatly across his chest. I paused briefly at the coffin and said my final goodbyes. Inwardly, the tears came.

That night, as I lay in bed, I realized we all die. My soul began to quiver. I didn't want my life to end. What if there wasn't a heaven? Maybe it's just over. Vanquished, I might end up sucked into a sea of perpetual nothingness—my spirit eclipsed into blackness forever. Shuddering, tears came. I asked God—if He is there—for help! No answer.

Near dawn, restless sleep finally came. As the sun rose, I awakened and was glad to still be alive. I sat on my bed, feet dangling over the edge. Eyes looking down at the floor, I remembered my fears from the night before. I thought of my deceased childhood friend again, knowing he wouldn't be in class today.

I dressed quietly, went downstairs, and ate my Fruit Loops. Another day for me. Not for my expired buddy. Not ever.

John D. Emens, PhD

4.54 Billion

Modern science has estimated that the earth is 4.54 billion years old. Yet, the scriptures report that the earth was made in one day—and the earth itself is just a few thousand years old. How do we reconcile this seeming great chronological difference? Can anything rationally explain such a temporal incongruence and empirical dissonance?

To begin to explore this chronological conundrum, we need to look at two important words. First, we need to define "day." Is a day twenty-four hours? Well, if we look at 2 Peter 3:8, we read, "But do not ignore this one fact, beloved, that with the Lord one day is like a thousand years, and a thousand years is like one day" (NRSV). The assertion here is that for God, there is no limitation vis-à-vis time or anything temporal as we understand it. For God, one day can be ten minutes or a trillion billion of our years. The second key word is "like." One "God day" may be like a million years, give or take a thousand here or there. God is not limited by time in any way. He can go back in time or forward to the future. Time is a human invention. So, when it says in the scriptures that the earth was created in one day, that could easily be four and a half billion of our years.

My dog Nika-boo is twelve years old. That makes her eighty-four years old in "dog years." The earth is four and half billion years old. That may make it one year old in "God years." Enough said.

THE BIBLICAL
CHASTISEMENT

An acquaintance once said, "My [Christian] God does not punish!"

However, it seems the Lord does dole out or allow a certain amount of suffering throughout the pages of the Bible. So, does God punish? The book of Lamentations 3:32–33 reads: "Although he causes grief, he will have compassion according to the abundance of his steadfast love; for he does not willingly afflict or grieve anyone" (NRSV). Yet, in Proverbs 3:11–12, it says, "My child, do not despise the Lord's discipline or be weary of his reproof, for the Lord reproves the one he loves, as a father the son in whom he delights" (NRSV). In Jeremiah 30:11, it reads: "But I will correct you in good measure and with judgment and will in no sense hold you guiltless or leave you unpunished" (Amplified). On the other hand, Nehemiah 9:17 states, "They refused to obey and were not mindful of the wonders that you performed among them. [B]ut you are a God ready to forgive, gracious and merciful, slow to anger, and abounding in steadfast love, and did not forsake them"(ESV). Psalm 103:10 states, "He does not deal with us according to our sins, nor repay us according to our iniquities" (NRSV). Job 11:6 says, "Know therefore that God exacts less of you than your guilt and iniquity [deserve]" (Amplified). It's almost like "good cop, bad cop." Who is the real God? Who is the "real" Yahweh? And where is the love of Christ in all of this?

At this juncture, it might be helpful to make a reference to what I saw on a Christian talk show about a guest who spoke of the efficacy of spanking their children. This parent called spankings a "biblical chastisement;" he argued "spanking" should be a last resort, but it should be done if a child commits a clear, harmful wrong. He believed a spanking should ensue if

John D. Emens, PhD

the child did something dangerous (like sticking a finger in an electrical outlet). This guest argued that children needed to learn an important lesson, namely, that there are consequences to their actions, good or bad. Modern psychology calls it positive and negative reinforcement.

I believe God treats us in a similar fashion. He does not want to "willingly afflict or grieve anyone" (as it reads in the aforementioned passage in Lamentations), but He loves us and is committed to our well-being. Just like our earthly parents, if we stray or go off course, He "corrects" us—gently at first, but also more strenuously if necessary. In a sense, God can be cruel to be kind to keep us on the straight and narrow. Some would call it godly "tough love."

In the scriptures, God does give "biblical chastisements" or spankings. For example, when David wrongly took Bathsheba, God forgave David's sin, but He still wouldn't allow the shepherd boy to build the Temple; that task was bumped down to his son Solomon. The grumbling, murmuring, ungrateful Israelites spent forty years in the desert before being allowed into the "promised land." Psalm 95:11 reads, "Wherefore I swore in My wrath they [the Israelites] would not enter My rest [the land of promise]" (Amplified).

Yet, God can be sweet and gladdening. In the book of Haggai, the prophet admonishes, but mostly encourages, the returning Israelite exiles to rebuild the Temple. They were dragging their feet, mostly concerned with fixing up their own "paneled houses." Through the words of the prophet Haggai (2:17), God asserted, "I smote you with blight and with mildew and with hail in all the [products of] the labors of your hands; yet you returned not nor were converted to Me, says the Lord" (Amplified). Even so, the Lord is gentle and encouraging to the slacking Israelites. In the book of Haggai 2:4–5, He says, "Be strong, alert, and courageous ... and work! ... fear not ... I am with you (1:13). From this day on I will bless you" (2:19) [all Amplified]. Here, God was kind, promising blessings if the Israelites changed their slothful ways.

Sweet Jesus? We know His kindness knows no bounds. He gave the thief on the cross the nod to come into "paradise" (heaven), just by acknowledging Him as God; He will do the same for us. In His anger, Jesus turned over the tables of the "money changers" and drove them out of the Temple for their unsavory activities. Then again, the resurrected sweet

Jesus forgave Peter for the fisherman's desertion of Him at the pivotal time of His capture and execution. Like Yahweh, or God Father, Christ seems to be hot or cold, depending on the situation.

At the end of the day, we see God is truly a person or persons (three in one). He has feelings, and He can be thrilled when someone comes to "know" Him. He can be hurt, discouraged, and disappointed when we sin or commit wrongdoings. He does reluctantly "correct" us. Whether we call that chastening a punishment depends one's point of view. As a child, my spankings were rare but necessary and not at all violent (mostly embarrassing). At age five, I once climbed out a second-story window onto a roof and received a necessary "correction" indeed.

The scripture says in Psalm 111:10: "The fear of the Lord is the beginning of wisdom" (NIV). Here, "fear" means reverence and respect. And truth be known, sometimes we all need a good "spanking" or two just to remind us who wears the pants in the universe.

THE POWER OF
THANKFULNESS

Paul writes in 1 Thessalonians 5:18: "In everything give thanks; for this is the will of God in Christ Jesus for you" (NKJV). The motivating word in this scripture passage is "everything." It is a simple command. In good times, be thankful. In bad times, be thankful. Even when times are uncertain or unclear, be thankful. This command by Paul is a bit murky in that we are usually used to expressing gratitude when we receive something positive, edifying, uplifting, helpful, or pleasing. But this isn't what is stated. We need to be thankful even in rough times and in tragedies and in times of loss, which is easier said than done!

Why be thankful in tragedy? Can you be grateful to God when your child succumbs to cancer at age six? In my case, can I be thankful or grateful in spite of losing my leg, my kidneys, my career, and my previous way of life? I can—and let me explain why. God's promises—His gift of eternal life through Christ—outweigh any bad or onerous earthly scenarios. It's hard, very hard, and when tragedy strikes, one (including myself) may have to go through the emotional progressions of grief. In other words, when bad news hits, we go through feelings of shock, anger, pain, acceptance, grief, recalibration, reconciliation, and redirection. After going through all these stages—I am sure there are more—we come to a place where we can take that deep breath and say, "Okay, God, I don't understand why any of this has happened, but I'm glad I have You to get me through this. I am thankful for Your promises and Your provision."

Imagine your seven-year-old boy falls off the backyard slide and fractures their arm. Very painful. He is screaming and crying. You hear his wails out back and look out the kitchen window. He is running toward the house holding his injured arm. You go to the back door and let him in. He runs into your arms, and you carefully examine him. You end up taking him to the nearest ER.

When he was wounded, he came to you, the parent. The child, boy or girl, could have been angry at you. After all, it was your slide and your house and your yard. They could have gotten mad and run as far away from you as possible. Yet, instinctively, they sought your help, knowing and trusting that you would help them in any way possible. In the heat of the moment, there was no discussion of who was to blame or why the injury occurred. Children love and need their parents. Parents love and look after their children. The bond between them is stronger than the trauma of the broken bone. After the ER, the parent takes the kid to McDonalds. The child kisses Mommy or Daddy and says, "Thanks!" The parent looks to the heavens and says, "Thanks!" It could have been much worse.

This little yarn has a happy ending. In life, there are not always happy endings. Years ago, a good friend told me she didn't believe in God. I asked her why, and she replied, "When I was in high school, my mom died of cancer. I stood there in the hospital room next to my mom, and as she was dying, I prayed, 'God, if you are there, please, please heal my mother.' And you know what? My mom died that day. That's why I don't believe in God. If there was a God, he would not have let that happen to my mother."

It was a very tough situation, but my friend was testing God before she had any kind of relationship with Him. She wanted God to do her will on her terms. When things didn't work out, she was done with God. Plain and simple. The real problem was that there was no bond between my friend and God that was stronger than the situation. My friend was using a healing as a litmus test for the existence of God—not as a trusting believer committing their parent into the healing hands of the Father come what may.

It is hard to be thankful when loved ones die or things go horribly wrong on many fronts. But thankfulness in the midst of tragedy is a form of spiritual maturity that does two things. One, it puts you in a much better position to pick up the pieces and move on. Second, it makes you that much more helpful to others and more useful to God when you, as Rudyard Kipling once asserted, can "keep your head when all about you are losing theirs."[22] There is power in thankfulness because gratefulness in trauma keeps us from collapsing under the weight of the bad circumstances. Like in sailing, the stronger the wind blows, the tauter you want your sail to push back against the wind in order to stay on course. Thankfulness to God in tragedy is keeping your sail taut through rough waters, and that is the best way to make it to safe harbor.

No one likes to experience challenging circumstances, but such circumstances will come. With thankfulness, we can endure tough times, and as it says in Matthew 24:13: "But he who endures to the end will be saved" (NKJV).

---

[22] Rudyard Kipling (1910) "If," first published in *Rewards and Fairies*.

FRONT PAGE

(Some thematic wrinkles in this essay came from a comic publication in the 1970s; all names and the story are purely fictitious).

It was a calm, cool, comfortable Connecticut morning. Belinda Jammer rested back easily in her crimson chaise lounge. She wrapped her hands around a warm, steaming mug of Folgers coffee. There was a slight frost on the windowpanes, and she was surrounded by healthy green plants; her favorite were the buxom Boston ferns hanging from the ceiling. Warm music oozed from the boom box at her feet; it was pumping out some spritely up-tempo Mozart.

Belinda contemplated her life. It had not been perfect. She knew she had made some mistakes. She regretted dropping out of school, marrying young, and having Jimmy at the age of nineteen. Divorcing Trace wasn't in the game plan, but when he went after that cocktail waitress, there wasn't much else to do. Belinda was just glad she got a good settlement and had invested the money wisely. She still felt bad that her twenty-five-year-old son was out of work and living at home. Jimmy never seemed to be the same after the breakup.

Her coffee had grown cold. When she went into the kitchen, her son was reading the morning newspaper. As she filled up her coffee cup, she noticed Jimmy's yellowed elementary school grade cards that were still taped to the refrigerator; they were all As. Belinda sighed. She knew she should someday take those old report cards down. She gingerly touched one and smiled. Then she glanced over at her son. He was tall, overweight, and tattooed, and he had a shaved head. Belinda sighed again. Jimmy had been such a good student and athlete before the divorce. It was too bad he had dropped out of high school. *What a shame*, she thought.

Before returning to the sunroom, Belinda glanced back at Jimmy. He was still reading the paper. Her eyes bulged, and her heart skipped a beat. "Jimmy! I am so proud of you!"

Not looking up from the paper, Jimmy dryly replied, "Why, Mom?"

Belinda bent over and wrapped her arms around her son. "Jimmy! When you were a child, all you looked at were the funnies. When you were an adolescent, all you looked at was the sports page. And now, finally, I see you reading the front page of the newspaper! You have finally grown up!"

"Yeah, Mom, I am reading the front page to see if any friends got busted." Jimmy smushed out his cigarette in a dirty ashtray.

Belinda's heart sank. She shook her head, took her coffee, and returned to the sunroom. As she lay back in her chaise lounge, she closed her eyes and wept silently. After a moment, she looked outside. The light snow had turned into a gentle rain. She longed for spring. Sadly, Belinda realized she had always longed for a lot of things.

Proverbs 22:6 says, "Train up your child in the way he should go; even when he is old he will not depart from it" (ESV).

THREE HARDEST WORDS

What are the three hardest words to say or swallow? I can think of four: "I need you," "I love you," "I forgive you," and "Your will be done."

First, we live in a world where we are supposed to be independent and self-sufficient. It is almost seen as a sign of weakness if we show need or vulnerability in any way. This is one reason why many people eschew religion. They see it as a weakness or a crutch. They say, "I don't need God." It is hard to believe in something you cannot easily see, but just because you can't visually see something, it doesn't mean you don't need it. We can't see air, yet we need it and breathe it. We don't usually see the benefits of our car or life insurance, yet we need them and pay for them monthly.

I don't really need my cell phone, but truth be known, I am almost scared to leave my home without it. We forget that it's okay to be vulnerable, admit our needs, and admit our imperfections. Philosopher Immanuel Kant reportedly said he had a vacant place in his heart that could only be filled with God. It's okay to be needy for God—He made us that way. It takes great strength to admit and voice our needs. Admitting and recognizing one's needs is like a lubricating moisture to leather; it makes it tougher, stronger, more flexible, more useful, and longer lasting. We should take note!

"I love you" is also very hard for some people to say. I am blessed in that I came from a family where those words were said daily. For me, saying "I love you" is more of a show of commitment than it is a feeling. For many people, commitment is scary. They may "love" pizza, football, or iced tea, but heaven forbid they say "I love you" to each other.

It takes courage to love and promise commitment to another. It takes courage to love your kids, your spouse, your friends, and other family. It takes courage and faith to love your God. Incipient in love is the fear of

John D. Emens, PhD

failure—the fact that whoever you love will not love you back. In effect, there is a fear of a broken promise—a breakdown of commitment from other people or from God. That's when we have to rely on the promises.

With God, our promises come in the form of scriptures. In 1 Chronicles 28:20, it says, "He will not fail you nor forsake you" (NASB). That doesn't mean it will be easy or that trouble will not come. It means that His commitment will not fail or waver. When we are in trouble, we have to show our commitment to Him to see how His commitment to us unfolds in His time and in His way. God is patient with us. We need to be patient with Him. He demonstrated His love for us by His Son's death, which gave us eternal life. His love is there for the asking; we just need to be willing to receive it.

"I forgive you" is another difficult phrase for many to say. When people hurt, wrong, or slight us, it can really, truly sting down deep. We may want retribution or revenge. It is easy to want to repay evil for evil, but the scriptures (Romans 12:21) instruct us to "overcome evil with good" (NIV). What is good? To forgive—even if we don't forget. To me, forgiving others is like when you take too big a bite of a peanut butter sandwich. You struggle to swallow it, and it's hard to get it down. You might need to drink some milk to do it. But when you finally do it—swallow it—you feel much better. When you have the courage to forgive others, you release them of their wrongdoing, and you feel better too!

Forgiveness is a double-edged blessing. They feel better, and you feel better. I have incurred serious wrongs from others in my life, and by forgiving them from the heart, I have released years of anger and resentment. I can testify that forgiveness can be a very freeing, strengthening, and an empowering thing.

"Your will be done" is actually four words, but they are just as hard to say and swallow. Look at Lord Jesus in Luke 22:42 when He was contemplating His crucifixion. Jesus did not want to die on the cross, but He said, "Father, if you are willing, take this cup from me; yet, not my will, but yours be done" (NIV). When you say those words, you are performing an act of deference. You are showing love and commitment to God by deferring your life, will, and choices to Him.

Nearly three years ago, I prayed to keep my leg, but I also said, "Your will be done." I eventually lost my leg. I prayed for my kidneys to be healed, but they still failed. Accepting bad or challenging circumstances isn't easy (and this is not to say all bad things are God's will), but turning over bad situations to Him and His will provides freedom and exudes trust. Implicitly when you say, "Thy will be done," you are admitting God knows things better than you. When the dentist painfully drills a hole in your tooth for a root canal, you are trusting that they know what they are doing better than you do. When going through a trial or testing period, by praying hard for resolutions to these challenges with "Thy will be done," you are letting God always play the final trump card. You let Him be boss.

"I need you," "I love you," "I forgive you," and "Thy will be done" are hard to say, but these words are the most powerful of all. Celebrated author Robert Parker once wrote, "Man afraid to die is a man afraid to live." The same could be said about those of us who are afraid to speak those three or four words.

Soft Hands

I have a vivid memory as a young child of asking my father for a drink of water while lying in bed in the wee hours of the night. He would come in to periodically check on me. If I was parched, he would bring in water to me carried in his cupped hands. Like a little bird, I would drink the water from his hands. His hands were gentle and soft (and hopefully clean).

In many ways, those early parent-child exchanges between my father and me were what bonded us so closely at an early age—and fully developed for the rest of our lives. Sometimes I fell or stumbled as a child and even as an adolescent, and when I apologized to my father, he would be quick to forgive. I was quick to recriminate myself for my mistakes, but my father would always remind me "to be gentle with myself" and that "nobody is perfect." His calming brow and gentle heart affirmed and supported me through good and difficult times, and the strength of our relationship gave me confidence to work hard and persevere with little fear of making mistakes. I learned that to err is only to be human.

I picture Father God and Jesus having soft hands. Yes, God is to be feared and respected, but Jesus has an incredibly tender side. His mercy is soft, genuine, and unrelenting. It reads in Isaiah 42:3 (and Matthew 12:20): "A bruised reed he will not break, and a smoldering wick he will not snuff out" (NIV). God loves us with a deeper love than any good father on earth possibly could. He made us, He created us, and He adores us. When we ask for forgiveness, He nods His head, places His holy hands around us, and gives us a huge hug. There is nothing deeper or more profound than the love of the Father. Amen.

FLEXING OUR
FAITH MUSCLES

Robert Murray McCheyne (2014) postulates that "faith is like a muscle." Faith only works through opposition. It only grows with pain. To "cultivate" faith, you must "challenge" it. Finally, if we don't flex our faith muscles, they become weak. In short, faith isn't a product—a thing to achieve or arrive at—it is an ongoing embattling process. The more your faith is confronted, provoked, and challenged, the deeper and stronger it will become.

How do we flex our faith muscles? How do we make them stronger? In the first place, we usually cannot and hope not to bring adversity upon us; life's tests will find us. But we can do four things to strengthen our faith. One, we can pray. Two, we can read scripture. Three, we can fellowship. Finally, we can serve.

When we pray, we thank God for His blessings, intercede for others in need, and listen for guidance. When we read the Word, we learn God's character and see how He acts in different situations with His people. With exegesis and isogesis, we relate the Bible to our everyday lives (pulling meaning out of the Bible and reading our world into the Bible). All the while, we read scripture to be ready to capture those aha moments that inspire and guide us. We fellowship to build up and edify each other. As Proverbs 27:17 reads, "As iron sharpens iron, so one person sharpens another" (NIV). Finally, to have a strong, practicing faith, we must actively serve—and serve with joy and gladness. James 2:17 reads, "In the same way, faith by itself, if it is not accompanied by action, is dead" (NRSV). And 2 Corinthians 9:7 explains that God likes a "cheerful giver" (NIV). Let us do our Christian service with light heart and good spiritedness. As we give, we too are edified. As Luke 6:38 reminds us, "Give, and it shall be given unto you" (KJV).

It should be recognized that in and of itself, having a good, strong, practicing faith in this modern, contemporary world is hard. Everything we see, touch, and taste—the empirical world—tells us there is no God. Yet, we can know God in our hearts and minds, and at times, we can feel His Spirit upon us. When He seems to "hide His face,"[23] we can trust in His promises and know His truth, His existence, and His faithfulness through a thorough knowledge of the scriptures.

When times get tough, we recount how He has delivered and strengthened us in the past, and we push through new adversities, knowing full well that overcoming these stumbling blocks will make us stronger. He will be there in times of trouble. As Dr. Derek Grier (2017) wrote, "If He leads you to it—He'll get you through it."

Hebrew 11:6 reads, "But without faith it is impossible to please him [God]" (KJV). This is all the more reason to daily hoist those barbells of faith to become spiritually stronger and more useful—and, most of all, to make our Maker proud.

---

[23] Psalm 10:1 and Psalm 88:14 (both NIV).

BIG FAITH CRUCIBLES

The crucible is for silver, and the furnace is for
gold, but the Lord tests the heart.
—Proverbs 17:3 (NRSV)

We all live in life's crucibles, and through them, good things can come. As toddlers, we fall and get up. In erring, we become corrected and thus smarter. Bringing bad water to a boil helps it become purified. Hefting dumbbells make us stronger. Falling off the two-wheeler teaches us riding skills. Raging forest fires bring forth the most fertile soils.

There are faith crucibles as well. Some are small faith crucibles, like believing you can jump rope, tie your shoes, or pass the next homeroom quiz. Then there are big faith crucibles, such as job loss, sickness, divorce, or the death of a loved one or of a child. The epistle of James 1:2 says, "Count it all joy, my brothers, when you meet trials of various kinds" (ESV). Sometimes I wonder if James wasn't talking about the trial-sized shampoo in roadside hotels and not tragedies as we understand them today. Trials can hurt, and hurt deeply, and the pain sometimes seems unending.

But James is right in that pain and suffering can and do make us stronger, helping us learn perseverance and patience. In doing so, our faith muscles are flexed and made stronger, more edified, and more fervent. Do not eschew or resent these tests; instead, embrace them. This onerous process gives us big faith. For this gift we can be thankful, and grateful as life's toughest crucibles melt, mold, and make us into mature, tested, useful, and wise ambassadors from above. Now passing these tests, we have a greater calling. Now we can better serve others.

John D. Emens, PhD

AFTERTHOUGHT

You shall not make a graven image [to worship
it] … You shall not bow down yourself to them or serve
them; for I the Lord your God am a jealous God.
—Exodus 20:4–5 (Amplified)

We know the Lord hates us worshipping idols. The infamous golden calf the Israelites worshiped and the priests of Baal on Mount Carmel come to mind. These are obvious, strident examples of idol worship. We can intuit God detests when we are infatuated with mammon since the scriptures say we can't love God and money; we have to make a choice. However, other forms of idol worship can creep in, and I am as guilty of this practice as anyone else. Let me explain.

I love college football. I am from Columbus, Ohio, and this is a college football town. On any week in autumn, by Thursday, I am chomping on the bit for football Saturday. Early in the wee hours of the morning on the sixth day of the week, I go to the grocery and gather all my game goodies, including snacks, drinks, and ingredients for homemade monster beef-and-cheese nachos. Twenty packs of chewing gum. Ingredients for homemade triple pepperoni, double-cheese pizza. Back home from the store by nine o'clock, I turn on ESPN's *College Gameday*, and my eyes are glued to the screen until the first game kicks off at noon. I subsequently go through twelve straight hours of football frenzy, only taking my eyes off of a game when I need to run to the kitchen for edible reinforcements. Yes, on Saturdays I live, eat, and breathe college football; it's really almost like an addiction.

Well, one late Saturday night last fall, I was resting after a long, rough day of football frenzy. My mind turned to what I was going to do on the following day, which was a Sunday. I noted that in the morning I was going to my men's group and then the church service. The more I thought about my plans for Sunday, I became convicted in the Spirit that something was wrong. I prayed to the Lord about what was amiss, and I sensed His deep disappointment with me. Then it hit me. He showed me that in my heart and mind, all my Sunday church activities were nothing more than an afterthought compared to my precious college football Saturdays. The scripture that came to mind was Exodus 20:3: "You shall have no other Gods before me" (ESV). Busted! I quickly repented and made amends.

Obviously, there are other sins much worse than being a football fanatic, but the Lord made His point. There are so many things we put before the Lord. Instead of praying, reading scripture, fellowshipping, and serving—spending time with and for Him—we fill our lives with distractions and other priorities that put Him second. As He has stated, He is a "jealous God." He wants to be number one, and He deserves to be numero uno. Unfortunately, we treat Him like He is second best or an afterthought. We forget He is a person (or persons, really) with feelings. When we ignore Him or make Him second best; it is truly unkind—and we come off as a bunch of ungrateful, unruly kids. Shameful indeed.

So let us remember what He has done for us! Let us put our idols down. Touchdowns count, but eternity counts more.

GRACE, MERCY, FAVOR, AND BLESSING

As believers in Jesus Christ, we talk a lot about grace and mercy. The simplest difference between the two is that grace is getting from God what we don't deserve (unmerited favor), and mercy is not getting what we do deserve. Regarding mercy, Job 11:6 says, "Know therefore that God exacts of you less than your guilt and iniquity [deserve]" (Amplified). In Psalm 103:9–10, King David writes, "He will not always accuse, nor will he harbor his anger forever; he does not treat us as our sins deserve, or repay us according to our iniquities" (NIV).

At the same time, it should be said that knowing and understanding God as a merciful God does not give us a free pass for sin and wrongdoing. Even though we know there is forgiveness and our sins are removed "as far is the east is from the west,"[24] we may still suffer serious or deleterious consequences for the wrongs we commit. As it says in Colossians 3:25: "For the one who does wrong will receive the consequences of the wrong that he has done, and that without partiality" (NAS). If we question this understanding, we have only to look at 2 Samuel 11–12. Although King David was forgiven for his adultery with Bathsheba and for setting up her then husband, Uriah the Hittite, for murder, King David suffered serious consequences. He lost his firstborn son by Bathsheba and was disallowed by God from building the Temple.

So, how do we, when doing wrong, find a way to elicit mercy from the Lord? The short answer is that we can't. Mercy and favor can only come by, and from, God alone. However, if we fear, respect, and exalt Him, the

---

[24] Psalm 103:12 (NRSV).

Lord seems to be more likely to bless us with more mercy. As it says in Isaiah 30:18: "And therefore will the Lord wait, that he may be gracious unto you, and therefore will he be exalted, that he may have mercy upon you" (KJV).

Furthermore, if we are humble, praise His name, and lift Him up, He is more akin to give us mercy and favor. As it reads in 1 Peter 5:15, "God opposes the proud but shows favor to the humble" (NIV). Amen and amen!

John D. Emens, PhD

TRUE HOME

Robert Frost, in the poem, "The Death of the Hired Man" (1914), wrote, "Home is the place where, when you have to go there, they have to take you in." We all have different conceptions and notions about home. For some of us, the term conjures up thoughts and feelings of love, security, and acceptance. For others, home might mean discord, disharmony, and perhaps emotional wreckage.

For all of us, the term home may be vastly different on many levels and in many ways. However, whatever our concept of home is here on earth, our true home is in heaven where we were once first conceived as an original thought by Father God. When we expire, heaven is where we will return because of and through the blood of Jesus Christ.

Frost's poem says, "When you have to go there, they have to take you in." In reality, we don't have to go to heaven, and they don't have to take us in. Some people may not want heaven for differing reasons; some persons may have notions that heaven is just a bunch of boring folks sitting around on a cloud for eternity. Many others believe that everyone gets to go to heaven. I wish this were true, but that isn't the case. In John 14:6, Jesus Christ said, "No one comes to the Father except through me" (NIV). Those are His words. Full stop.

Those who don't know Christ will go elsewhere, and as for where this might be, I take my leave; that locale is totally up to Him. What I do know is that for those who know Christ Jesus, their names are written in the Book of Life. They do go to heaven. Those of us who are "written in" have a guaranteed room reservation for a mansion in the sky and a seat at the supper table for the feast of the Lamb. It has been said that in heaven, Father God has a new name for each one of us, and we certainly know not what all the goodies "God prepared for them that love Him."(1 Corinthians 2:9 ASV).

In Betty Eadie's *Embraced by the Light* (1992), she takes the reader through her journey to heaven via a near-death experience. In her visit, she makes several observations such as that in heaven, we will all have a variety of jobs, and that Jesus Himself is a sheer entity of pure love and brilliant light. For me, heaven will be spending much of eternity being able to sit and gaze at the face of the Father in awe and splendor for a very, very long time; this is my utmost desire.

For all of us, I firmly believe heaven will be pretty much like what the singer-songwriter Jimmy Buffet said about his infamous song "Margaritaville." "It's anywhere you want it to be." For some people, heaven is playing golf on gorgeous greens and splendid fairways. For others, it may be extended vacations walking barefoot on soft, sandy beaches or munching on a variety of succulent foods unending (we will actually eat in heaven—recall how Jesus ate fish in front of the disciples after His resurrection). There may be many faraway places to visit, and who knows what planet we may choose to set up our camping tents. It boggles the mind just to ponder what might be and where we will go. Heaven will be more than we can now possibly imagine.

Apostle Paul said in Philippians 1:21: "To live is Christ and to die is gain" (NIV). I firmly believe what he meant was "to live" is "to suffer," as did our Lord; "to die" is "to go someplace better." Life is hard, and we do suffer down here on earth, but when we pass away, we will go to a more beautiful, unfathomable, unimaginable place. As for heaven—like Saint Paul—I can't wait to get there! I look forward to seeing you there as well! Amen and amen!

Epilogue

A lot has happened in the past three months. On February 4, I received a kidney transplant from a deceased donor at Ohio State-Wexner Medical Center in Columbus, Ohio. So far, the kidney is functioning well; my incision line has healed, and my lab numbers are good. Glory to God!

I was on dialysis for two and a half years. Lots and lots of prayers and God's grace and mercy can only explain the blessing of receiving this gift from this deceased donor. I am so grateful to the Lord Jesus Christ for this amazing blessing; I now have a second chance at life. It was truly an arduous waiting game; dialysis is tough, but I am so grateful in that it kept me alive long enough to obtain the kidney.

This all brings up the topic Christian author and speaker Evangeline Colbert (2018) discussed regarding delayed versus denied blessing. She makes reference to 2 Corinthians 1:20: "For all the promises of God find their yes in him. That is why it is though him that we utter Amen to God for his glory" (ESV). In this passage of scripture, we note that all God's promises end in yes. We know we have a faithful God even if things happen in His time and not necessarily in our time. God always fulfills His promises if we are patient and let things play out His way. As it says in 1 Kings 8:56: "Not one word has failed of all the good promises he gave through his servant Moses" (NIV).

So, we know God's good promises are true and will come to fruition. We should note the aforementioned passage in 2 Corinthians 1:20, "It is through him that we utter Amen to God for his glory" (ESV). We want and need to understand that in all His answered promises, He gets all the glory.

Jesus had heard of his friend Lazarus's sickness, yet in John 11:4, it reads that the Lord promised, "This sickness will not end in death. No, it is for God's glory so that God's Son may be glorified through it." (NIV). Here is where delayed, not denied blessings, are really exemplified. The Lord Jesus waits two extra days after of hearing of Lazarus's sickness before He actually departed to be with his ailing friend. Jesus allowed Lazarus to die so that He could later resurrect him "so that God's Son may be glorified."

Many times, the hardest part is waiting for God's promises to come to fulfillment. We must be faithful as we wait for the Lord to deliver us. As it says in Galatians 6:9: "And let us not be weary in well doing: for in due season we shall reap, if we faint not" (KJV). It tests our faith as we wait for God to act. Continue to pray and believe. We must also continue to seek Him. As it says in Hebrews 11:6: "But without faith it is impossible to please him: for he that cometh to God must believe that he is, and that he is a rewarder of them that diligently seek him" (KJV).

So, take heart. Even when it looks like things will take forever or that things might not work out, have faith in God's promises. Good things will happen with patience and long-suffering. As it reads in Psalm 37:9: "But those who wait for the Lord shall inherit the land" (NRSV). And never, ever forget what it says in 1 Corinthians 13:8: "Love never fails" (NIV).

BIBLE VERSIONS USED IN THE TEXT

Amplified Version (Amplified)
American Standard Version (ASV)
Contemporary English Version (CEV)
English Standard Version (ESV)
International Standard Version (ISV)
King James Version (KJV)
New American Standard Bible (NASB)
New International Version (NIV)
New King James Version (NKJV)
New Living Translation (NLT)
New Revised Standard Version (NRSV)

CPSIA information can be obtained
at www.ICGtesting.com
Printed in the USA
BVHW030823181121
621922BV00001B/1